RESEARCHER COACH

RESEARCHER COACH

A Personal Guide to the
Research Journey

Ximena P. Suárez Sousa
Boyd L. Bradbury

LEXINGTON BOOKS/FORTRESS ACADEMIC
Lanham • Boulder • New York • London

Published by Lexington Books/Fortress Academic

Lexington Books is an imprint of
The Rowman & Littlefield Publishing Group, Inc.
4501 Forbes Boulevard, Suite 200, Lanham, Maryland 20706
www.rowman.com

86-90 Paul Street, London EC2A 4NE, United Kingdom

British Library Cataloguing in Publication Information Available

Library of Congress Cataloging-in-Publication Data

Names: Suárez Sousa, Ximena P., 1968- author. | Bradbury, Boyd L., author.
Title: Researcher coach : a personal guide to the research journey / Ximena
    P. Suárez Sousa, Boyd L. Bradbury.
Description: Lanham, Maryland : Lexington Books/Fortress Academic, [2022] |
    Includes bibliographical references and index. | Summary: "The book
    provides sufficient theoretical and practical support so that readers
    gain a sense of self-direction and autonomy as they navigate their own
    research journeys"—Provided by publisher.
Identifiers: LCCN 2022015268 (print) | LCCN 2022015269 (ebook) | ISBN
    9781475861839 (Cloth : acid-free paper) | ISBN 9781475861846 (Paperback
    : acid-free paper) | ISBN 9781475861853 (ePub)
Subjects: LCSH: Social sciences—Research.
Classification: LCC H62 .S7965 2022 (print) | LCC H62 (ebook) | DDC
    001.4/2—dc23/eng/20220524
LC record available at https://lccn.loc.gov/2022015268
LC ebook record available at https://lccn.loc.gov/2022015269

For my 16-year-old daughter Misqa,
an avid reader and evidence seeker who (at this stage
of her development) does it mostly to prove me wrong.

—Ximena Suárez Sousa

For my late parents, Leslie "Bud" and Genevieve Bradbury,
who instilled in me the value of education and hard work.

—Boyd Bradbury

"Nothing in life is to be feared, it is only to be understood. Now is the time to understand more, so that we may fear less."

—Marie Curie

CONTENTS

List of Illustrations   ix

Foreword   xv

Preface   xix

Acknowledgments   xxiii

1 Introduction to Research   1

2 Writing the Introduction   21

3 The Literature Review   43

4 Methodology   67

5 Writing the Results   99

6 Writing the Discussion   119

7 Qualitative Research Designs   133

8 Quantitative Research Designs   153

9 General Research Items   181

10 Conclusion   187

References   191

Index   205

About the Authors   209

ILLUSTRATIONS

FIGURES

1.1   Research paradigm: terms and relationship   3

2.1   Very relevant literature   24

2.2   Conceptual framework   32

5.1   Figure example   108

5.2   Figure with photo   109

5.3   Process of data analysis   112

5.4   Conceptual map   113

5.5   Figure example of score distributions   116

5.6   New conceptualization diagram   117

8.1   Boxplot   156

8.2   Bar Graph   158

8.3   A-B-A-C design   159

8.4   Scatterplot   161

8.5   Pie chart   163

TABLES

1.1　Research Paradigms　4

2.1　Recommendations for Writing Research Questions　35

4.1　Research Paradigm: Ontology, Epistemology, Methodology, and Methods　74

4.2　Brief Description of Qualitative and Quantitative Research Designs　75

4.3　Components to Calculate Sample Size When Comparing Two Means　83

4.4　Sampling Types　84

4.5　Types of Variables　87

4.6　Research Question(s) Alignment　96

5.1　Participant Demographic Data　110

5.2　Qualitative Data Example 1　111

5.3　Qualitative Data Example 2　111

5.4　Descriptive Statistics　114

7.1　Site Four Analysis　148

8.1　Calculation of Return Rate　165

8.2　Threats to the Internal Validity of Quantitative Research Designs　166

8.3　Formulas to Calculate Sample Size　170

8.4　Important Elements to Consider When Calculating Sample Size　171

8.5　Commonly Used Inferential Statistics by Quantitative Research Design　175

TEXTBOXES

2.1　Introduction Paragraph　23

2.2　Introduction Paragraph with Headline　23

2.3   Brief Literature Review   25

2.4   Statement of the Problem   27

2.5   Parent–School Engagement   28

2.6   Theoretical Framework   31

2.7   Purpose of the Study: Summer Slide   33

2.8   Purpose of the Study: Rubrics   33

2.9   Quantitative Research Questions   36

2.10   Qualitative Research Questions   36

2.11   Definition of Variables: Quantitative Design   38

2.12   Significance of the Study   38

2.13   Limitations of the Study   41

2.14   Delimitations of the Study   41

3.1   Cultural Factors from the Preliminary Report:
           Comprehensive Study of Education and Related Services
           on the White Earth Indian Reservation   47

3.2   White Earth Study Topical Outline   60

4.1   *Summer Slide Study: Partial Statement of the Problem*   69

4.2   *Summer Slide Study: Partial Purpose of the Study*   69

4.3   *Summer Slide Study: Research Questions*   70

4.4   Research Design Statement: Qualitative   76

4.5   Research Design Statement: Mixed Methods
           Sequential Explanatory   76

4.6   Research Design Statement: Mixed Methods   76

4.7   Setting Description: Corporate Learning Environment   78

4.8   Setting Description: Public School   78

4.9   Participants Description   79

4.10   Participants Description: Youth   80

4.11   Participants' Inclusion and Exclusion Criteria   81

4.12   Sample   82

4.13   Population Description   85

4.14   Variables Description   88

4.15   Measurement Tools   88

4.16   Validity Study Plan   90

4.17   Reliability Study Plan   91

4.18   Research Questions   95

5.1   Referencing a Table in Parenthesis   107

5.2   Referencing a Table in Text   107

5.3   Narrative of Results   114

6.1   Overview   121

6.2   Findings and Conclusions   125

6.3   Limitations and Delimitations   126

6.4   Recommendations   129

6.5   Recommendations for Future Research   130

6.6   Conclusion   132

7.1   Narrative Inquiry   137

7.2   Research Design Rationale   139

7.3   Grounded Theory Description   140

7.4   Research Design Rationale Relative to Other Designs   140

7.5   Contribution of Case Study Research Design   141

7.6   Case Study Rationale   142

7.7   Data Analysis Spiral Method   145

7.8   Deductive Coding (A Priori Codes) and Open and
          Axial Coding, Part 1   145

7.9   Deductive Coding (A Priori Codes) and Open and
          Axial Coding, Part 2   146

7.10 Deductive and Inductive Coding   147

7.11 Rationale of Open, Axial, and Selective Coding   149

7.12 Process of Open, Axial, and Selective Coding   150

8.1   Sampling Procedure   172

9.1   Abstract   183

FOREWORD

Maria D. Vásquez-Colina

Having designed and taught research methods courses for almost two decades gives me the opportunity to see research in action, like when students or colleagues put together a project. My own research inquiry regarding assessment literacy and research capital, especially with a focus on culturally and linguistically diverse communities, gives me a chance to collaborate with community members.

When asked to write this foreword and after reading this book, I thought of the importance of "experiencing research." Allow me to expand. I first met Ximena Suárez Sousa when we were in second grade in primary school in a small town in Peru. She was a new student in my school. While first encounters vary, this one was memorable. We exchanged a few words and toured our small-town school located near the Peruvian Andes foothills. We asked each other questions and laughed. There was joy and curiosity in those learning experiences. Since then, we have exchanged more than a few words. We have had parallel and interconnected academic journeys in higher education in the United States. First, it was my good fortune to land a graduate assistantship at the University of Louisville. It happened to be that Ximena was also completing her graduate studies there. Thus, we were able to support each other's academic efforts and expand our curiosity of wanting to know more in our fields. While we went separate ways after graduating, the inquiry bond and friendship strengthened throughout the years. When Ximena and I became assistant professors and taught research methods–related courses at Minnesota State University–Moorhead and Florida Atlantic University, respectively, we discussed our courses curricula, our teaching methods, and how best to support our students learn about research. The same discussion has continued since our promotion and tenure process.

To navigate the academic world, one shall create spaces to dialogue, to ask questions, and to reflect. These spaces include scholarly peer-reviewed conferences where we present a paper and exchange feedback. As scholars, Ximena and I presented at the American Educational Research Association (AERA) Annual Meeting on various occasions. These meetings provided us with opportunities to network and continue our conversations. It was there where Ximena introduced me to Boyd Bradbury, who served as the dean of the College of Education at MSU at that time. These three-party, long conversations would include views on different educational topics including our teaching, our research projects, and our service to our community. And, let me tell you, if you have attended a professional meeting before, you know that these academic rendezvous become a highlight of those scholarly meetings. Boyd's accounts of his work in Minnesota were really impressive. Having lived myself in Minnesota for a while, his narration and his research interest added to what I thought I knew of the area and of the field of educational leadership.

Those of you who teach research methods or are learning about research methods know that a research topic could not be easily understood due to the terminology, procedures, and/or lack of experience learning about and conducting research. In this textbook, the use of practical examples like when the authors refer to the Little Havana best restaurant, provides a rich context to research. Their clear explanation of notions of integrity and rigor in research makes the reading flow effortless. And if the reader has wondered about different paradigms, epistemologies, ontologies, and axiologies, this book offers a rich buffet of clear and differentiated notions from where to select and feed your inquiry hunger. The thorough discussion on how to frame a research question to be the driving force of a research study is critical to the understanding of the research methods.

In my view, the different sections of the book are aligned to research methods courses and research proposal sections, such as distinguishing the theoretical or conceptual framework and setting the delimitations of the study as well as discussing the implications. The authors' direct communication style suggests to the readers a friendly conversation, like if you would be at your adviser's or colleague's office discussing research methods. Furthermore, the use of current examples from students' dissertations adds significance and realism to their words.

As you read, you will hear Ximena and Boyd talk directly to you. Their emphasis on research ethics provides critical knowledge and discussions to enrich your inquiry. The explanation of what involves writing a literature review and their examples of annotated bibliography are helpful pieces of information to start creating your own.

Throughout the textbook the authors engage in a dialogue. In my opinion, this style empowers the reader with knowledge. As I often discuss in my research, one needs to be literate in research to become good consumers of research and engage in research; I call this "research literacy." When the author talks to the readers asking them to ask questions and be critical, and the reader engages in those activities, research "magic" happens. That is, you become curious and engage in inquiry. Those are perfect research skills to have.

In sum, reading this book has been really a pleasure, and it has provided context and meaning to the different parts of a research proposal. I know firsthand that coming up with a research problem is not an easy task. It takes time, and it is a process. This book can be a useful tool to go through the process. This is Suárez Sousa's and Bradbury's book of research methods. I am extremely proud of being part of this book venture through the stories and this foreword. I am honored to be associated with this successful writing effort and wish Ximena and Boyd best of luck in what I believe could be many future editions. I can't wait to see it published and recommend it to students and colleagues.

PREFACE

This first edition of *Researcher Coach: A Personal Guide to the Research Journey* has the goal of providing specific guidance to first-time social science researchers on each of the critical steps required for the successful completion of their scholarly projects. This book was not written for the consummate researcher; on the contrary, this book was written for practitioners becoming researchers at some point in their careers. Specifically, we wrote this book having in mind practitioners who are leaders in their respective disciplines and who have the privilege of tackling social issues in which they are ongoingly immersed and about which they can do something transformational through their visionary applied research. This book was inspired by our doctoral students, who are committed practitioners holding positions of leadership in the K–12 and higher education settings. Their respective doctoral journeys stimulated us to produce a resource that could be instrumental in developing a solid understanding of what is required when planning and carrying out rigorous and meaningful research.

With *Researcher Coach: A Personal Guide to the Research Journey*, the reader will be able to answer some critical questions that impact their scholarly work. Specifically, is the social phenomenon of interest able to be researched? What is the research paradigm, and to which paradigm does my research belong? What are the fundamental differences between ontology, epistemology, methodology, and methods? Which research methodology best fits my research question? Which methods can be utilized to collect and analyze qualitative and quantitative data? How are results presented? What are the strategies used when discussing the results and recommendations for practice? Finally, the most significant question of all is, "Can I do this on my own?" The truth of the matter is that while the research journey can feel like a daunting endeavor, it has been carried out for centuries, ever since Francis Bacon wrote his *Novum Organum* (1620) and created a revolution to the established approach on how to study and interpret natural phenomena. Our book will help the reader understand what the scientific method entails, gaining a sense of confidence to carry on their research project while focusing on one step of the process at a time without losing track of the big, systemic picture.

Researcher Coach: A Personal Guide to the Research Journey has some unique features. First, we provide real samples from past and recent scholarly work to illustrate each and every step of the research journey. Second, the book is written following the writing sequence of a scholarly work; that is, we have chapters that provide guidance on how to write the introduction, the literature review, the methodology, the results, and the discussion and recommendations for practice. Third, there are additional chapters providing more in-depth understanding on specific components of the research process (e.g., qualitative designs). In all, the book follows the sequence of the scientific method without losing sight of the systemic thinking that researchers must possess when framing their inquiry. Because each chapter was written in a way that can be read independently, the reader should be forewarned that there is some unavoidable redundancy when reading the entire book.

We had the idea of writing this book a few years ago, and the idea became more relevant as we transitioned into teaching exclusively in the educational leadership doctoral degree program. This was the right time to write it. Both of us have worked in academia and have been engaged in research for a combined span of four decades. Our career roots are in teaching and learning. Ximena came to the United States in the 1990s, having worked as an educational psychologist in her native Peru, and Boyd was a Spanish teacher who became a school principal as well as superintendent prior to moving to higher education, where he also held the position of faculty dean for a number of years. Currently, we are professors at Minnesota State University Moorhead; Ximena is the coordinator of the Educational Leadership Doctoral Program and Boyd is the chair of the Department of Leadership and Learning. We are also editors of the *Interactive Journal of Global Leadership and Learning*, a scholarly peer-reviewed journal currently in its third year of operations. We felt compelled to write this book feeling confident of our knowledge and experience with research, and we also realized there was a need for a book like ours, one that could coach practitioners through their research journeys.

As we write the preface, the world continues to face the COVID-19 virus that triggered the worst global pandemic of the century and that started almost two years ago: a natural challenge that has placed a tremendously unexpected burden on leaders and workers across all industries. While problem-solving under duress posits significant challenges, thinking within the parameters of the scientific method helps individuals remain problem-focused rather than emotion-focused, largely contributing to the identification of the most appropriate solutions to problems. As researchers, we are committed to service. In March 2020, at the dawn of the pandemic, we conducted an expedited study to identify the most impending issues that teachers in Minnesota were facing, personally and professionally (Bradbury et al., 2020). This was a critical and timely study whose findings were broadly disseminated across the state educational administrators and contributed to the triaging process of local schools under such a large crisis. We hope our book will support other researchers to carry out their call for service to their respective communities, tackling important social phenomena under any and all circumstances.

Researcher Coach: A Personal Guide to the Research Journey is not designed to be an exhaustive book on how to conduct research nor to be a book that simply supplies the reader with basic knowledge of the topic. Our book provides the reader with substantial content and guidance so that the research planning and execution can be conducted with validity and rigor. While many studies have a team of researchers (e.g., *Comprehensive Study of Education on the White Earth Indian Reservation*, by Bradbury et al., 2010), researchers working on their own should remember that consulting with peers is an instrumental part of any researcher's journey and growth, particularly when egos are humble and service is the focus. If the researcher is a master's degree or doctoral student, the main consulting individual should be the chair of the thesis or dissertation committee. If the researcher is a practitioner or faculty member, capitalize on self-direction and self-agency, as these are expected attributes of adult learners. In this age of easy access to scholarly information from an array of platforms, researchers have the ability of studying on their own and continue learning independently while also consulting with peers or colleagues as needed.

While researchers should not feel paralyzed or unequipped to do their job, they should remember that learning will never cease, and it will always be an innate part of the research endeavor. The scientific method is a knowledge-generating tool not continuously changing as knowledge itself does. The scientific method helps us know *reality*, making it one of the greatest tools to humanity's disposal. Because of that, researchers must respect the process and never cease to learn and prepare for the challenges brought up by the vast social phenomena of our era. We hope *Researcher Coach: A Personal Guide to the Research Journey* will play an important role in coaching researchers through their scholarly and learning endeavors. We learned quite a bit thanks to this writing journey, and we sincerely hope we will be able to guide the reader through the process of generating new knowledge on the social issues that are of high importance to their communities.

ACKNOWLEDGMENTS

We would like to express our utmost appreciation to a number of individuals who were pivotal in the development of *Researcher Coach: A Personal Guide to the Research Journey.*

We would like to start with our doctoral students. Their journey was ours from the inception of the doctoral program in educational leadership at Minnesota State University Moorhead (MSUM) back in 2017. The convergence of their inquisitiveness, our teaching strategies, and mentoring styles generated the idea of writing a book that could accompany any individual journeying through the rigorous but gratifying process of doing research for the very first time. For us, it is a privilege to work in higher education and an honor to serve our students.

We are also thankful to the MSUM community of scholars that continuously challenges us to embark on worthwhile academic projects. In particular to our dean, Dr. Ok-Hee Lee, and our closest colleagues in the Department of Leadership and Learning. Special thanks go to our team of reviewers, who took charge of selected chapters and provided the meaningful feedback from the perspective of practitioners who had recently completed the doctoral journey. Their contributions were invaluable: Dr. Angela Brekken, dietetic dietitian program director at Northland Community and Technical College; Dr. Abigail Bremer, assistant professor of education at Valley City State University; Dr. Jeff Burgess, superintendent of the Mesabi East School District; Dr. Noelle Green, principal of Watford City Middle School; Dr. Rachel Hunt, assistant professor and chair of the Kinesiology and Human Performance Department at Valley City State University; Dr. Kyja Kristjansson-Nelson, professor of film at Minnesota State University Moorhead; Dr. Laurie Larson, academic dean at Rasmussen University; Dr. Patria Lawton, assistant professor of communication studies at Inver Hills Community College; Dr. Elizabeth McMahon, e-learning higher education consultant; and Dr. Kathrina O'Connell, assistant professor of professional education at Bemidji State Minnesota.

Researcher Coach benefited from the pivotal book editing contributions of Dr. Tiffany Bockelmann, adjunct professor of education in the Educational Leadership Program at Minnesota State University Moorhead and associate editor of the *Interactive Journal of Global Leadership and Learning*. Her tireless, diligent, prompt, and thorough editorial work ensured our book was correctly formatted and responsibly cited.

Finally, we would like to thank our families. This project was accomplished to large extent because we had them cheering us up no matter what, along this great writing journey.

❶

INTRODUCTION TO RESEARCH

This chapter is intended to give a basic overview of research principles and components. Research can take many forms, so it would be foolhardy to attempt an exhaustive explanation of research in a single chapter. Instead, this chapter will highlight the basic components of research, which include paradigms, epistemology, ontology, axiology, research design, theoretical perspectives, methodology, and methods, and it will endeavor to serve as a primer and guide for those who want to conduct research and aspire toward scholarship.

This chapter, combined with Chapter 4, should prove helpful in obtaining a basic understanding of paradigms, epistemology, ontology, axiology, research design, theoretical perspectives, methodology, and methods for those seeking to conduct research.

RESEARCH IN A NUTSHELL

Within a layperson's lexicon, *research* means simply that someone is looking into something. Within the academic world, however, *research* conveys a systematic approach toward the study of a topic, replete with specific research questions and a correspondingly appropriate methodology. These questions and associated methodology are situated within a paradigm (viewpoint or belief system), epistemology, ontology, theoretical framework, and conceptual framework that must tie together in an intelligible way. To ask 10 friends as to the best Cuban restaurant in Little Havana is not research; instead, it is the solicitation of opinions. If one truly wanted to know the best Cuban restaurant in Little Havana, one would need to determine whether there is a single truth as to the best restaurant, how one would go about knowing that truth, what constitutes truth, and the best overall approach, including methods for gathering and analyzing data. To determine the best Cuban restaurant in Little Havana, it is doubtful that one would find a single truth. For some, price would matter. For others, quality would be the only criterion in determining the best restaurant. For still others, price, quality, service, location, and other considerations would come into play. If, however, one wanted to know the most expensive Cuban restaurant in Little Havana, there likely would be a single truth. The research approach and associated components necessary to determine the most expensive Cuban restaurant in Little Havana would be quite different than the one used to determine the best restaurant.

The thing about research is that it must have integrity to constitute legitimate research. One can't just go about willy-nilly looking into something and call it research. Integrity means that all parts of the process must hold together to produce an end product that can be viewed as valid or trustworthy. Just as a house must have a solid foundation, the correct construction (e.g., building, electrical, plumbing, and heating and cooling systems), and trained contractors to produce a good end result, so must researchers utilize the correct components as trained professionals to produce findings that are worthwhile and trusted.

RESEARCH PARADIGMS—WHY THEY MATTER

For the beginning researcher, the term *paradigm* may be an unfamiliar one. With that noted, one's paradigm is important since it frames one's research. A research paradigm can be defined as the manner in which research evidence might be "understood, patterned, reasoned, and compiled" (Morrison, 2012, p. 16). In other words, at the onset of research, researchers must think about what specific questions they are attempting to answer, the best approach by which these questions can be answered, and the basic framework or context within which the research should be viewed. In a nutshell, it is the research question or hypothesis that drives a research project. A paradigm, for all practical purposes, is the lens or viewpoint through which a researcher will conduct research.

Paradigms are varied, and it must be understood that paradigms, epistemologies, ontologies, axiologies, methodologies, and methods must align for research to be viewed as valid or trustworthy. Scott and Morrison (2006, p. 170) highlighted four paradigms within research as follows:

Positivism/empiricism, where it is accepted that facts can be collected about the world; language allows us to represent those facts unproblematically; and it is possible to develop correct methods for understanding educational processes, relations and institutions.

Phenomenology as a form of interpretivism, where the emphasis is placed on the way human beings give meaning to their lives; reasons are accepted as legitimate causes of human behavior; and agential perspectives are prioritized.

Critical theory, where it is accepted that values are central to all research activities; describing and changing the world are elided; and the researcher does not adopt a neutral stance in relation to the world.

Postmodernism, which rejects universalizing [sic] modes of thought and global narratives; understands knowledge as localized; and seeks above all else to undermine the universal legitimacy of notions such as truth.

It should be understood that there is a connection between and among paradigms, epistemologies, ontologies, axiologies, theoretical perspectives, methodologies, and methods. This connection is illustrated in figure 1.1, and an expanded list of paradigms and the connection to aforementioned items are found in table 1.1.

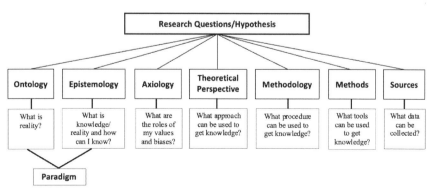

Figure 1.1. Research paradigm: terms and relationship.
Adapted from Brown & Dueñas (2020), Creswell & Poth (2018), and Patel (2015).

Table 1.1. Research Paradigms.

Paradigm	Ontology	Epistemology	Axiology	Theoretical Perspective	Methodology	Method	Sources
	Reality	*Knowledge*	*Value/Bias*	*Approach*	*Procedures*	*Tools*	*Data*
Positivism	• Single reality	• Reality can be measured through valid and reliable tools to produce knowledge	• The researcher's biases are controlled, not expressed in the study	• Positivism • Post-Positivism	• Experimental research • Survey research • Quasi-Experimental • Correlational • Causal-Comparative • Single-Subject	• Usually quantitative • Sampling • Observation • Measurement • Statistical analysis • Questionnaire • Focus group • Structured interview	• Pre-post test • Exam Scores • Rating Scales
Constructivism/ Interpretivist	• Multiple realities constructed through lived experiences	• Knowledge is subjective and formed at an individual level • Reality co-constructed between researcher and the researched	• Individual values are honored and negotiated among individuals	• Reality needs to be interpreted • Phenomenology • Symbolic Interaction-ism • Hermeneutics (See also Critical Inquiry)	• Ethnography • Grounded Theory • Phenomenology • Case Study • Heuristic inquiry • Action research • Discourse analysis	• Usually qualitative • Interview • Observation • Participants and Non-Participants • Case Study • Life History • Narrative • Theme Identification	• Audio and Textual data from interviews • Field notes • Document analysis • Open surveys

Pragmatism	• Reality is continually renegotiated, debated, and interpreted according to new/unpredictable situations in order to be useful	• The best method is one that solves problems as change is the underlying aim • Reality is known using both deductive and inductive forms of evidence	• Values are discussed because of the way knowledge reflects both the researcher's and the participants' views	• Deweyan Pragmatism • Research through design	• Mixed methods • Design-based research • Action research	• Uses both qualitative and quantitative approaches • Expert review • Usability testing • Prototype	• Any from positivism and/or constructivism
Subjectivism	• Reality is what is perceived to be real • Emergent Subjective-objective reality	• Multiple ways of knowing • All knowledge is purely a matter of perspective	• Values need to be problematized and interrogated • Respect for indigenous values	• Postmodernism • Structuralism • Post-Structuralism	• Discourse theory • Archaeology • Genealogy • Deconstruction • Collaborative • Questioning of methods	• Auto-ethnography • Semiotics • Literary analysis • Pastiche • Intertextuality	• Documents • Artifacts • Observations • Interviews
Critical Inquiry	• Reality is socially constructed • Power and identity struggles • Privilege oppression based on race, ethnicity, class, gender, mental abilities, sexual preference	• Reality and knowledge are both socially constructed and influenced by power relations within society	• Diversity of values is emphasized within the standpoint of various communities	• Marxism • Queer Theory • Feminism • Critical Race Theory • Disability Theory	• Critical discourse analysis • Critical ethnography • Action research • Ideology critique	• Ideological review • Civil actions • Open ended interviews • Focus groups • Open-ended questionnaires • Journals	• Audio and Textual data from interviews • Field notes • Open surveys

Adapted from Brown & Dueñas (2020), Creswell & Poth (2018), and Patel (2015).

What must be understood about paradigms is that the perspective of the researcher matters; that is, what does the researcher hope to accomplish? If one were interested in bringing about change and convinced that truth is constructed through social interactions, then a critical paradigm would be appropriate. On the other hand, if a researcher were convinced that absolute truths can be discovered in the world with no tolerance for qualitative interpretation, then a positivistic paradigm should be selected. Paradigms, however, can be viewed on a spectrum in that researchers can be flexible in approaching research. A pragmatist views reality as negotiable and interpreted and therefore, researchers should use whichever methods are available to best answer the research question. Whichever one's chosen paradigm, the key is making certain that there is agreement across the key elements that were mentioned in figure 1.1 and table 1.1. Additional information regarding paradigms and their relationship to epistemology, ontology, methodology, and methods can be found in the research design section of Chapter 4 of this book.

ONTOLOGY, EPISTEMOLOGY, AXIOLOGY, AND RESEARCH QUESTIONS—WHY THEY MATTER

Ontology and *epistemology* are not commonplace in the common English lexicon. These terms, however, are key to researchers. In a nutshell, epistemology is how we know what we know, and ontology is what we know. Morrison (2012) explained,

> Epistemology, then, is central to research endeavor. All researchers ask questions about knowledge—how we find it, how we recognize it when we find it, how we use it and how it distinguishes truth from falsehood. In other words, researcher seek to "know" the "reality" they are describing. Educational researchers bring a wide range of theoretical perspectives to their work. Perhaps the widest of these is ontology. This consists of a range of perceptions about the nature of reality and is important because it affects the way in which researchers can "know." Together, ontology and epistemology affect the methodologies that underpin researchers' work: methodology is based upon critical thinking about the nature of reality and how we can understand it. (p. 15)

Axiology refers to one's values and beliefs. Tomar (2014, p. 51) explained, "Axiology focuses on questions about what 'ought to be.' It deals with the nature of values and relates to the teaching of moral values and character development." Tomar continued,

> Values guide our decision as to what is good, true and right. Thus they depend as much on your feelings as on our thoughts. These values include the simple difference between right and wrong, a belief in God, the importance of hard work, self-respect. (p. 52)

As a researcher, what must be remembered is that one's values are bound to shape one's perspectives and viewpoints. As a result, axiology plays a role in our paradigm choice, it influences what one sees as truth, and it impacts the means by which one arrives at truth.

One consideration related to axiology within qualitative research, especially phenomenology, is *epoché*. In a nutshell, epoché, also known as bracketing, involves the setting aside of biases and assumptions in research to arrive at the truth of a phenomenon. By following practices associated with epoché, one can help to address bias. Bednall (2006) addressed epoché by noting,

> My major challenge then in seeking an authentic phenomenological method, was the design of a particular mechanism which enabled me to be aware of my own potential for bias, how to suspend that bias at the commencement of data collection, and then use an explicit process to evaluate the significance of that bias in data interpretation. There needed to be a functional symmetry between myself and the research focus and then a structural relationship between myself and the data under examination. (para. 15)

Central to the discussion of paradigms, epistemology, ontology, axiology, theoretical and conceptual perspectives, and methods is the research question(s). In research, the interrogative is in many ways the force that drives the overall study. It is likely fair to note that one's paradigm or epistemological and ontological viewpoints influence the questions one would ask, but there is certainty that the research questions influence the choice of paradigm, epistemology, and ontology—closely tied components of research. In returning to the Cuban restaurant example used earlier in this chapter, while not impossible, it would be difficult to utilize the paradigm of positivism, which subscribes to a single truth that can be quantitatively measured through validated instruments, to determine the best Cuban restaurant in Little Havana. "Best" is a rather vague term that could mean different things to different people. While one could administer a questionnaire with a scale from best to worst and let patrons mark their appraisal, other paradigms would reveal, in all likelihood, a more complete understanding of what patrons would mean as best or worst. As a result, the paradigms of constructivism/interpretivism, pragmatism, or subjectivism would seem better choices (see table 1.1).

Similar to the Cuban restaurant example, to make sense of research, one could consider assessment, which is of utmost importance within the educational realm. The evaluation means utilized to assess a student's proficiency with an outcome needs to match the intended outcome. For example, if one thinks about the English fable *The Three Little Pigs* (Galdone, 1970), a multiple-choice test would be perfectly fine if a teacher wanted students to demonstrate basic recall/knowledge, the lowest level of Bloom's Taxonomy (Anderson et al., 2001) regarding main characters, plot, and setting. A multiple-choice test simply gives the student an option to select a correct answer that would be factual in nature. If, however, a teacher wanted students to evaluate (a higher level of Bloom's Taxonomy) the moral characters of the three pigs and the wolf, a multiple-choice test would not suffice. A teacher would need an essay response of some sort to properly assess the student's response. In evaluating the moral character of the three pigs and the wolf, one would look for far more than a basic fact; one would need to see supporting evidence for an argument. The basic idea of appropriate assessment tied to outcomes can be transferred to the concept of research; that is, whatever the question, it must align with an appropriate paradigm, epistemology, ontology, axiology, theoretical perspective, methodology, and vice versa. Is there a single truth, or can there be multiple truths? Is reality what one perceives it be based upon one's own judgment, or is there no room for negotiation? Is truth individualized, or is it a matter of social construct? The bottom line is that research questions drive a researcher's perspective and a researcher's perspective helps foster the research questions that are asked.

THEORETICAL PERSPECTIVES DEFINED

A *theoretical perspective* is the approach one uses to know something. One's perspective comes part-and-parcel with the other key research components—paradigm, epistemology, ontology, methodology, and methods. At the highest level, one's theoretical perspective is influenced by the fundamental belief that truth is either objective or subjective. In other words, one either believes that truth can be verified independent of what one perceives or experiences or one believes that truth is derived from individual perception, social interaction, or experiences. Frequently utilized theoretical perspectives are herein listed with condensed explanations.

Positivism

Positivism is a theoretical perspective that subscribes to the belief that there is an objective, single truth that can be discovered through research. Positivism is associated with quantitative research. According to Greenwood and Levin (2000, p. 92), "Positivistically-based quantitative researchers employ the language of objectivity, distance, and control because they believe these are the keys to the conduct of real social science."

Post-positivism

Post-positivism is usually associated with quantitative research, and post-positivist researchers derive knowledge from: determinism or cause-and-effect thinking; reductionism, by narrowing and focusing on selected variables to interrelate; detailed observations and measures of variables; and the testing of theories that are continually refined (Slife & Williams, 1995). Those who subscribe to post-positivism tend to involve some degree of interpretivism from sources such as text data (e.g., open-ended question responses) in addition to quantitative data.

Interpretivism/Constructivism

Interpretivism or constructivism is most closely associated with qualitative research. Creswell and Plano Clark (2007, p. 22) explained that constructivists understand the meaning of phenomena "through partici-pants and their subjective views." Participants draw their understandings from their own personal histories, which include interactions with others.

Critical Inquiry

Critical inquiry is associated with qualitative research and subscribes to the beliefs that reality and knowledge are socially constructed and influenced by the power dynamics present in a setting. Mason (2018, p. 8) defined this perspective as determining life "through social and historical processes and power relations—researcher seeks to uncover these and question the taken-for-granted." Fay (1987) and Morrow and Brown (1994) explained further that while there are variants of criti-cal theory, it tends to focus on the study of social institutions and their transformations through interpreting the meanings of social life; the historical problems of domination, alienation, and social struggles; and a critique of society and the envisioning of new possibilities.

Feminism

Feminism is most closely associated with qualitative research, and it focuses on gender. Creswell (1998, p. 83) noted, "The theme of domi-nation prevails in feminist literature as well, but the subject matter is gender domination within a patriarchal society. Feminist research also embraces many of the tenets of post-modern critiques as a challenge to current society." Oleson (1994) explained that the goals of feminist research involve the placement of the researcher within the study so as to avoid objectification, and to conduct transformative research."

Pragmatism

Pragmatism is often associated with mixed methods research since this viewpoint utilizes whichever methods help to answer a question. Hibberts and Burke Johnson (2012, p. 124) noted that pragmatism "is a popular philosophy in mixed research." Creswell and Plano Clark (2007, p. 23) explained further, "The focus is on the consequences of research, on the primary importance of the question asked rather than the methods, and multiple forms of data collection inform the problems under study." Pragmatists are not searching for absolute truths, but rather the best means (qualitative and quantitative) to collect data and support findings. Unlike those who either support or reject positivism, researchers who subscribe to pragmatism view knowledge as both a human construct and the product of reality beyond human construct. In the view of pragmatist researchers, at least some truths are fluid.

Postmodernism

Postmodernism is associated with qualitative research, and it manifests itself in select theoretical perspectives, such as critical inquiry and feminism. It should be noted, however, that those who subscribe to research perspectives, such as critical inquiry and feminism, that aim to bring about change as a result of research, do not necessarily view themselves as postmodernists. According to Thomas (1993), postmodernism is characterized by a number of interrelated characteristics, which include the attempt to influence those who accept established theories and beliefs. Additionally, Bloland (1995) noted that postmodernists challenge established meta-narratives and theories. This challenge may attempt to simply change minds rather than bring about actual change. Mason (2018) emphasized that postmodernists, post-structuralists, and anti-foundationalists provide a "challenge to the authority of established rational theories and their claims to 'truth' and expertise, disputes the idea that there is one truth or reality—researcher aims to deconstruct established ways of knowing and dominant interpretations and discourses." In a nutshell, postmodernists do not believe that the world can be depicted through the accumulation of evidence to establish a single truth or reality.

Structuralism

Structuralism is associated with qualitative research, and it examines individual elements for interrelationships and patterns within larger systems. Heydebrand (2001) defined structuralism:

Structuralism is an intellectual tendency that seeks to understand and explain social reality in terms of social structures. Structures are defined as the patterns and forms of social relations and combinations among a set of constituent social elements or component parts such as positions, units, levels, regions and locations, and social formations. (p. 15230)

Nel (2016) explained further the interplay of parts within a system:

> Structuralism is a form of critical research. It focuses on the systems (structures) within society and the power relations within and among the parts (subsystems) as a whole. In formalised structures, one can easily see the hierarchy of positions and levels of power. In utilising structuralism as a research method, the channels of power are laid bare as the researcher critically analyses and maps the relations and interplay among the parts. Structuralism does not emphasise the uniqueness of each of the parts, but rather seeks to reveal how some common aspects of the parts relate those parts to the larger whole. Structuralism posits that no part in a particular system has any significance in and of itself—its identity is defined in terms of its relationship between all the parts of the system. (para. 2)

Post-structuralism

Post-structuralism is often, but not exclusively, associated with qualitative research, and it can include various theories. The main idea of post-structuralism is that meaning does not exist outside of the text and that meaning is not fixed but rather contingent and unstable. Grogan and Cleaver Simmons (2012, pp. 31–34) suggested that post-structuralism and postmodernism are essentially synonymous. Grogran and Cleaver Simmons noted that many feminist researchers have been inspired by postmodern/post-structuralist ideas. In post-structuralism, meanings of social phenomena are constantly changing, reassessed, and unstable. According to Olssen (2003, pp. 192–193), Michel Foucault is one of the most famous post-structuralists in that: he rejected the notion central to structuralism as a system of universal rules or laws or elementary structures that underpinned history and explained it in surface appearances; he stood opposed to a marked tendency amongst structuralist writers to prioritizing the structure over the parts, or the preexistence of the whole over the parts, whereby the units can be explained once the essence of the structure is uncovered; and he believed structuralism failed to theorize adequately the historicity of structures.

Queer Theory

According to Gamson (2000, p. 348), "The study of sexualities in general, and homosexualities in particular, has long been closely intertwined with qualitative research." Queer theory is a relative newcomer in regard to theoretical perspectives. Its origins are likely derived from gay and lesbian studies of the late 1980s and 1990s (Hostetler & Herdt, 1998). According to Grogan and Cleaver Simmons (2012, p. 36), "Derived from a postmodernist deconstruction of the stable identity, queer theory calls into question and problematizes such binary constructions as straight/gay and male/female. That sexuality is naturally, as opposed to socially, produced is also critiqued." Grogan and Cleaver Simmons (pp. 36–37) added, "Informed by poststructuralist and feminist theories, queer theory centres on the notion of sexuality to challenge the restrictive and damaging heteronormative and homophobic social order."

Critical Race Theory (CRT)

CRT is associated with qualitative research, and it gets at the idea that racism is an inherent and accepted part of society. CRT contends that racial inequality between races emerges from the social, economic, and legal differences created by Whites to perpetuate an economic advantage and maintenance of power at the expense of minorities. Ladson-Billings (1997) explained,

> Critical race theory (CRT) first emerged as a counter legal scholarship to the positivist and liberal legal discourse of civil rights. This scholarly tradition argues against the slow pace of racial reform in the United States. Critical race theory begins with the notion that racism is normal in American society. It departs from mainstream legal scholarship by sometimes employing storytelling. It critiques liberalism and argues that Whites have been the primary beneficiaries of civil rights legislation. (p. 7)

Grogan and Cleaver Simmons (2012, p. 35) noted that "institutionalized racism is a very important understanding brought to the fore by CRT." Additional tenets of CRT include: 1) interest convergence, which emerges from a Marxist view that the proletariat will only benefit from legal advances if the bourgeoisie stand to gain more power and privilege; and 2) there is value in narratives and counter-stories (Grogan & Cleaver Simmons, pp. 35–36).

METHODOLOGY AND METHODS— DISTINCTION AND RELATIONSHIP

Methodology and *methods* seem to be used interchangeably by many, but in reality, these two terms, while interrelated, have different meanings. Methodology is the process, means, or manner by which one goes about finding the answer to a research question. More specifically, a methodology refers to the philosophical framework and the basic assumptions of research (van Manen, 1990). Methods (see table 2.1) are the tools or techniques used to gather the data for analysis. Creswell (2003) added that methods are specific in that they are techniques of data collection and analysis.

Methodologies are many and varied. As a result, several of the most utilized methodologies are listed below with condensed explanations.

Survey Research

If one were to ask people how they knew something, many would likely note that a "survey said" x, y, or z. Surveys and corresponding results are seemingly everywhere. Mujis (2012, p. 140) noted that "survey research is one of the most widely used research methods in the field of educational leadership, and certainly the most used quantitative approach." Mujis further explained,

> Survey research is a method of collecting standardized data from a large number of respondents. Survey research designs are characterized by the collection of data using standard questionnaire forms. The key element of survey research is standardization. In a survey, we will ask the same questions to all respondents. Survey research, if the sampling framework is appropriate, also allows us to collect data that we can gerneralise [sic] to a population. (p. 140)

It should be noted, however, that survey research is not exclusively quantitative in nature. Qualitative researchers conduct survey research via interviews and open-ended questionnaires. In addition, surveys are often part of mixed methods research, but they must be done correctly. Creswell and Plano Clark (2007) noted the importance of sampling and survey design to yield valid and/or trustworthy results.

Ethnography

Ethnography is associated with qualitative research. The traditional approach to ethnographic research involves "the researcher putting themselves physically and synchronously into a setting or site, and being involved in or observing its dynamics" (Mason, 2018, p. 139). In an age of technology, however, the approach to ethnography has changed for some. According to Pink et al. (2016), digital or online ethnography has taken root. No longer is physical placement necessary to observe the dynamics of social interaction and the impact of a setting or site. One thing that the COVID-19 pandemic has shown is that many endeavors once considered the exclusive domain of physical presence can be accomplished virtually (e.g., focus groups via Zoom.com).

Grounded Theory

Grounded theory is associated with qualitative research. Grounded theory is attributed to Glaser and Strauss (1967). Although not always in agreement, Glaser and Strauss (1999) provided an updated account of how to conduct grounded theory as years progressed. It is generally accepted that grounded theory derives its name from the practice of generating theory from research that is grounded in data (Babchuck, 1996).

Coding is a key aspect of grounded theory, and the process is time consuming. According to Bradbury (2005, p. 71), "At the heart of grounded theory analysis, the researcher uses a coding process that consists of three types: open, axial, and selective." Kristjansson-Nelson (2020a) provided an extensive explanation of grounded theory, replete with schools of grounded theories, processes, and procedures, including coding, and an application of grounded theory for those researchers who want to understand an inductive approach to research as theory emerges from data.

Phenomenological Research

Phenomenological research is associated with qualitative studies. According to Mason (2018), phenomenology involves the world, consciousness, perception, and lived experiences as inseparable. For those who subscribe to phenomenology, "there is not an objective world that exists separately from our perception of it—researcher needs to explore this interconnectedness" (p. 8). Morrison (2012) added,

> From the writings of the "father" of phenomenology, Albert Schultz (1967), and from recent proponents, comes the view that "the phenomenologist attempts to see things from the person's point of view" (Bogdan & Taylor, 1975, p. 14). The emphasis is upon how people in educational settings build understandings of their world by continually trying to interpret sense data. Reality is viewed as a social construction. In recent years, it is a research position inhabited most closely by those who follow critical and postmodernist schools of thought. (p. 21)

Action Research

Action research can be associated with quantitative, qualitative, and mixed methods studies. If ever there were a methodology designed for practitioners, it would be action research. Action research, in a nutshell, involves the identification of an issue in need of change, an intervention that addresses that issue, and measurement to see whether the intervention had an apparent impact on the issue. Hinchey (2008) summarized the basic components of action research as follows:

- It is conducted by those inside a community (teachers, administrators, community members) rather than by outside experts.
- It pursues improvement or better understanding in some area the researcher considers important.
- It involves systematic inquiry, which includes information gathering, analysis, and reflection.
- It leads to an action plan, which frequently generates a new cycle of the process. (p. 4)

Stringer (2007) added a succinct definition of action research:

> Action research is a systematic approach to investigation that enables people to find effective solutions to problems they confront in their everyday lives. Unlike traditional experimental/scientific research that looks for generalizable explanations that might be applied to all contexts, action research focuses on specific situations and localized solutions. Action research provides the means by which people in schools, business and community organizations; teachers; and health and human services may increase the effectiveness of the work in which they are engaged. (p. 1)

Bona fide action research projects at schools located on the White Earth and Red Lake Indian Reservations in Northwestern Minnesota serve as examples of action research projects that were implemented by practicing teachers. Bradbury (2011a) reported that these projects

> varied considerably by grade level and discipline, but all had as their common aim the strengthening of student learning or improvement of the classroom climate. The five projects documented in this issue of *Thresholds* aptly illustrate the varied achievements and interests of the participating teachers. They range from introduction of an animal to improve classroom climate (Peterson) to use of technology to enhance high school choral instruction (Jirava). Also included are a study of spelling instruction designed to improve the fluency of student writing (Schoenborn), support for self-directed learning in online courses (Wothe), and introduction of guided reading in a remedial primary classroom (Refshaw). (pp. 7–8)

Mixed Methods Research

Mixed methods research, as the name aptly implies, involves both quantitative and qualitative research. Creswell and Plano Clark (2007) described mixed methods research as follows:

> Mixed methods research is a research design with philosophical assumptions as well as methods of inquiry. As a methodology, it involves philosophical assumptions that guide the direction of the collection and analysis of data and the mixture of qualitative and quantitative approaches

in many phases of the research process. As a method, it focuses on collecting, analyzing, and mixing both quantitative and qualitative data in a single study or series of studies. Its central premise is that the use of quantitative and qualitative approaches in combination provides a better understanding of research problems than either approach alone. (p. 5)

Hibberts and Burke Johnson (2012, p. 122) added that "mixed research is the paradigm that systematically combines aspects of quantitative and qualitative research methods into a single study to take advantage of each paradigm's strengths."

While the employment of mixed methods can be beneficial, there are caveats. On one hand, mixed methods research can provide more extensive findings. Since quantitative research tends to produce the what, and qualitative research produces the how and why, one can get more robust findings through mixed methods research. On the other hand, mixed methods research is more time consuming since one must conduct varied research avenues and approaches. Moreover, mixed methods research requires varied expertise. Oftentimes, it is easier to conduct mixed methods research as a team; that is, with others who have complementary expertise.

Discourse Analysis

Discourse analysis is associated with qualitative research, and it shares select commonalities with structuralism and post-structuralism. Discourse is a key aspect of Foucault's work, in which he suggested that the "judges of normality are everywhere" (Foucault, 1977, p. 304). According to Perryman (2012, p. 312), "Simply put, discourse analysis is about uncovering the socially constructed context in which words are spoken and written." A central part of discourse analysis is the focus on power relations and political dynamics that are omnipresent in organizations and society as a whole. Perryman noted,

If we accept that discourse is a framework in which society works, then discourse analysis can be defined as an examination of data in order to gain familiarity with the social processes behind the words. As Phillips and

> Hardy (2002, p. 2) argued: "without discourse there is no social reality, and without understanding discourse we cannot understand our reality, our experiences, or ourselves." (p. 312)

Within discourse analysis, there are different approaches or areas of focus. Some researchers tend to focus on social order aspects that are influenced by discourse, while others look at everyday life, such as actions and talk, to determine the importance of what constitutes normal for individuals and groups. With that noted, in general, discourse analysis accepts words and behavior as central to what constitutes norms within social, political, and organizational settings. Gubrium and Holstein (2000, p. 490) emphasized that ethnomethodologists, who study how social order is produced in and through processes of social interaction, "focus on how members actually 'do' social life, aiming in particular to document how they concretely construct and sustain social entities, such as gender, self, and family."

Feminist Standpoint

The feminist standpoint is associated with qualitative research. According to Grogan and Cleaver Simmons (2012),

> The basis of feminist standpoint theory is that all knowledge is dependent on the social and historical context of the individual knower. In other words, an individual's standpoint influences her knowledge of the world and her standpoint is shaped by the economic and political situation in which she is situated. (p. 32)

Postmodern ideas have served as a catalyst for many feminist standpoint research studies. Feminist theories often explore the question of power within the context of gender, racial, socioeconomic, and sexuality contexts. Oleson (1994) provided various strands that represent the complexity of feminist qualitative research. These strands included: writings by women of color; problematizing unremitting Whiteness; postcolonial feminist thought; lesbian research and queer theory; disabled women; standpoint theory; and postmodern and deconstructive theory.

CONCLUSION

This chapter highlighted the basic components of research, which included paradigms, epistemology, ontology, theoretical perspectives, methodology, and methods. This chapter served as a primer and guide for those who want to conduct research and aspire toward scholarship. Condensed definitions of paradigms, axiology, theoretical perspectives, and methodologies were provided as a starting point for those pondering research possibilities and approaches. This chapter, combined with Chapter 4, should provide solid guidance in regard to the varied and stimulating world of research.

2

WRITING THE INTRODUCTION

The writing of scientific content demands the sustained utilization of *expository* discourse, which favors "academic or more literate language registers" (Silliman et al., 2019, p. 2). In linguistics, a *register* represents the "functional varieties of language operating in different contexts of use" (Matthiessen & Kashyap, 2014, p. 1). That is, individuals adjust their written or spoken linguistic features (e.g., vocabulary, syntax, discourse) according to their audience and the surrounding circumstances (e.g., conference presentation, describing the study to a childhood friend while eating pizza). Because the goal is to write scientific content to an audience of scholars, the chosen linguistic features must remain associated to the professional discipline or disciplines to which the content connects and these features should also reflect a higher level of language construction.

While there are many issues to keep in mind when writing, citing, and formatting scholarly content (e.g., avoid colloquialisms, contractions, and anthropomorphisms), the main guide should be the citation style associated to the researcher's own discipline. For example, in education and psychology the guidelines from the American Psychological Association (APA) are used. Professionals in the humanities (e.g., modern languages, literature, philosophy) follow the guidelines from the

Modern Language Association (MLA), while those in business follow the Chicago Manual of Style. Researchers must follow the appropriate guidelines as well as distinctive writing features observed while reading the literature—that is, the focus is on how ideas are communicated and how language is utilized (e.g., active voice, tense). In the end, the writing will reflect the researcher's own style, but this person needs to also make sure the requirements of authoring scholarly content are met. All in all, scholarly writing is a privilege that researchers must use well. This chapter provides guidelines to write each element in the introductory chapter or section.

This chapter will review the following components: introduction, brief literature review, statement of the problem, theoretical or conceptual framework, purpose of the study, hypothesis and research question(s), definition of variables, significance of the study, ethical considerations, and delimitations and limitations of the study. Researchers should keep in mind that there must be consistency across all of these components (Newman & Covrig, 2013); that is, researchers must pay attention to the terms used to ensure the narrative is consistent and that there is no switching to synonyms across methods, variables of study, or even research questions (e.g., parenting, parenting style, or style of parenting).

INTRODUCTION

What is the phenomenon the researcher is studying? The introductory text of a dissertation, manuscript, or technical report is a critical component as it provides the first encounter with the phenomenon of interest. "It basically sets forth the research problem and why it is important to be studied" (Creswell & Clark, 2011, p. 256). In that sense, the researcher should start the introduction by providing broad background information about the phenomenon (e.g., summer slide) and defining it broadly in terms of its impact to a specific group of individuals (e.g., elementary students' regression of learning). While the researcher will not be writing explicitly about what the plan for the study is, the researcher needs to establish the overall need to study this phenomenon. Researchers need to keep in mind that the introduction is also the best opportunity to capture the readers' attention about how relevant a study on this phenomenon would be considering their own professional practice and/or research interest. The introduction should leave the reader trusting that in the

---

TEXTBOX 2.1.

Introduction Paragraph

Educators return to school in the fall, energized to meet their new groups of students and eager to build upon students' learned skills. Students' skills in September, however, are not always what they were in May. Some skill scores stay the same or increase, but many scores decrease during the summer months. While this does not affect the teachers' commitment to differentiate instruction and guide students to success, the learning trajectories of many students are reversed.

---

scholarly work they are about to read, they will gain understanding of tools or models for the practice of their profession that serves the communities affected by this phenomenon or expand their understanding of existing theories regarding this phenomenon (Abramson, 2015). Textbox 2.1 (O'Connell, 2020, p. 1) shows the first paragraph of an introduction that presents the problem without naming it (i.e., summer slide).

The author clearly and succinctly depicts what this phenomenon represents to the individuals directly impacted by its occurrence and sets the context for the reader to recognize the urgent need for proposing and testing some solutions. Likewise, take a look at textbox 2.2 (Cummings, 2020, p.1). This is another example of the role that the introductory text plays in generating immediate understanding about how further study is relevant and needed to benefit the individuals affected by the phenomenon of interest. Once again, the goal is to write a compelling depiction of the phenomenon and how it impacts certain groups of individuals.

TEXTBOX 2.2.

Introduction Paragraph with Headline

"Teachers are screaming out" reads the headline of a recent article in the *Fargo Forum* (2019, May 14, 6:11 PM). It is a negotiation year for the Fargo Public School District (FPSD), and, in an unusual turn, teacher pay was not the forerunner of negotiation topics during the most recent teacher negotiation meeting with FPSD's Board of Education. Rising concerns about students' physical aggression was the top concern for teachers. The local news article stated that "there were 630 student behavioral issues in which a staff member was injured" in the 2018–2019 school year. A previous *Fargo Forum* article (2019, Apr 29, 9 PM) shared that 70% of teachers indicated they are "fearful in their classrooms" and "facing violence regularly because of student behavioral problems." These articles are becoming prolific as teacher contract negotiations continue. This district is not, however, alone seeing a rise in such student behaviors. Reported by KGW8 (2019, May 1, 10:22 AM), Oregon teachers are leaving the classroom due to increasing verbal and physical student behaviors in general education classrooms. In this article, teachers cite a lack of support being the reason for their exodus from the classroom.

BRIEF REVIEW OF THE LITERATURE

What do we *already know* about this phenomenon? This brief review serves the purpose of providing succinct background information and context to better understand what is the phenomenon of interest and also the significance of the researcher's inquiry, which will come later (i.e., significance of the study). This section synthesizes and systematizes what Rudestam and Newton (2001) called the *very relevant literature* (see figure 2.1), that is, a presentation of the most significant research findings and historical events directly associated to the chosen topic, the phenomenon of scholarly interest that drives the study.

The main idea is to describe what is known about this phenomenon, who are affected by it, what historical events contributed to its development, what solutions or approaches have been tried by experts in the field during the past few decades, as well as the outcomes. This section should include "key terms, ideas, theories, vocabulary" associated to this

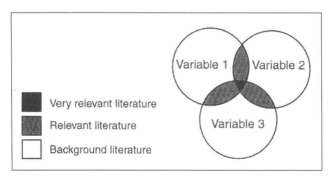

Figure 2.1. Very relevant literature.
Source: Rudestam & Newton (2014, p. 64).

field of study (Grant & Osanloo, 2014, p. 19). While this sounds like a lot of information to condense, the researcher needs to carefully select a few seminal studies and historical events that help to succinctly, but unequivocally, demonstrate not only that the researcher is knowledgeable about this phenomenon but that this is also something important to be studied.

A well thought out list of keywords, which are usually collected during preliminary readings (Creswell, 2014), will help the researcher conduct an exhaustive search of the most relevant primary and secondary sources. It is good practice to start this process by reading seminal primary sources; these articles contain a list of references that need to be further explored. Researchers can collect in this fashion primary and secondary sources theoretically and methodologically linked to the phenomenon of interest. When writing, researchers must always begin with the most general historical antecedents and end with specific studies that directly relate to their own, as in Kuhn's *paradigm funnel*, which is described in great detail by Berthon et al. (2003). It is discouraged to describe or summarize studies or historical events one by one in a linear manner. The writing must produce a well-articulated and systematized new scholarly piece that is multidimensional and connects many components at the same time.

This brief review of the literature should anticipate a) the need for conducting the study and b) the assurance that the study will fill some important gaps or deficiencies in the existing literature in terms of knowledge. In other words, the researcher needs to explain what still needs to be researched. Textbox 2.3 (Bradbury et al., 2020, p. 6) provides a sample of the historical context of a study exploring the personal and professional challenges experienced by teachers as they navigated the beginning months of the school closure crisis that resulted from the COVID-19 pandemic of 2020.

TEXTBOX 2.3.
Brief Literature Review

Although natural disasters and illnesses are part of life's fabric, the pervasiveness and breadth of the COVID-19 pandemic are defining features that set it apart from most crises that have impacted the world, and most specifically, the United States. The most relevant comparison of the COVID-19 crisis is the 1918 influenza pandemic, and the most recent comparison involves the HINI influenza pandemic. According to Swaggert et al.

(2020), "The COVID-19 lengthy school closure and crisis are unprec-
edented. Minnesotans have had school closures due to blizzards, floods,
fires, tornadoes and school shootings, but these closures were always in
specific geographic areas affecting limited numbers of students for limited
time periods. (Wong et al., 2014) The Spanish flu of 1918–19 which killed
over 10,000 Minnesotans resulted in school closures of several weeks but
was not a state-wide closing. Schools closed to limit the spread of the
virus but students did not have the opportunity to continue their studies.
Teachers were often asked to volunteer to help brining health and sanitation information to families and the community (Stern et al., 2009). In
2009, the H1N1 influenza pandemic resulted in sporadic Minnesota school
closures with outbreaks in certain school districts resulting in short-term
closures. However, hygiene emphasis, health monitoring, and ill student
quarantines were more often utilized (Como-Sabetti et al., 2010). The
spring 2020 COVID-19 worldwide pandemic and resulting shutdown of
schools and businesses and stay at home orders for all citizens is a first
for Minnesota and the United States" (p. 1).

While the researcher will later write a more extensive review of the
literature, this brief review needs to focus on the most seminal as well
as chronologically comprehensive studies.

STATEMENT OF THE PROBLEM

Is there really a need for the study? The researcher needs to state the
essential facts that cement an unequivocal justification as to *why* additional research on this phenomenon is important. What is still concern-
ing the researcher? For example, the researcher may be interested in
studying the impact of this phenomenon on a population that has not
been included in the literature (e.g., foreign immigrants with doctoral
degrees and low English proficiency). The researcher may also desire
to explore an aspect of the phenomenon that may not be commonly addressed by the research community (e.g., the manifestation of seasonal
affective disorder in countries within the equatorial latitude). There
may be a need to develop new tools to measure the phenomenon (e.g.,
validation of the Braille version of a self-appraisal instrument on self-
efficacy) or an interest to challenge the existing theories that explain
this phenomenon (e.g., Bandura's theory of social learning). Because the

researcher has already presented the gaps and deficiencies of the existing literature (Creswell & Clark, 2011), a context for the *why* of further research was created, and now it needs to be explicitly stated. The narrative should also help the reader entertain the idea of what could be the potential consequences of not conducting this study.

Also, it is very critical that the language used in writing the statement of the problem "foreshadows the tradition of inquiry" (Creswell, 1998, p. 94). This means the narrative should help the reader deduce what is the researcher's lens. The language used by a positivist, pragmatist, or interpretivist researcher when describing a given phenomenon of interest is quite different from each other. Information on the traditions of inquiry (i.e., researcher's lens) can be found in other sections of this book (i.e., Chapters 1 and 4). Textbox 2.4 (McMahon, 2021, p. 5) shows a statement of the problem for a study focusing on online instruction and higher education faculty, and textbox 2.5 (Leland, 2020, p. 3) presents the statement of the problem for a study that focused on parent–school engagement with a sample composed of Somali parents.

TEXTBOX 2.4.
Statement of the Problem

It is unknown if faculty who are designing and teaching online courses are accurately assessing their skills and abilities to do so effectively. Inaccurate self-perception may lead these faculty to forego professional development opportunities that would support their professional growth and development in areas where it is most needed. It is also not known if certain types of professional development are more likely to lead to course design improvements that are consistent with what is known about effective online course design practices. Professional development meant to prepare novice and experienced higher education faculty to design and teach effective online courses is not always provided in formats and times that are convenient for faculty, and it is not known if what is offered leads to the intended outcome of improved courses. Additionally, there are instances where faculty who have a high sense of self-efficacy are taking a "do it yourself" approach to learning how to design and teach online courses or who have developed their own set of best practices to follow in the design of their courses. Taken together, this uneven and potentially lacking preparation to teaching online may leave faculty without the requisite skills or knowledge necessary to create online and blended courses that support student learning and success.

> ## TEXTBOX 2.5.
> ### Parent–School Engagement
>
> Current research has recognized considerable benefits of parent and family engagement with their children's schools (Fan & Chen, 2001; Henderson & Berla, 1994; Hill & Tyson, 2009; Jeynes, 2003; Wilder, 2014). However, research shows many systemic and individual barriers to effective parent and family engagement (Ahmed, 2017; Baker, Wise, Kelley, & Skiba, 2016; Epstein, 2019; Jeynes, 2011). Located in a rural Minnesota setting, Fairbault Public Schools (FPS) has a large population of Somali refugee parents with limited English proficiency. Based on data from FPS, children from these families are falling behind in school. The FPA system has acknowledged the need to enhance engagement with these families to more effectively support their children's success in school.

THEORETICAL AND CONCEPTUAL FRAMEWORKS

How is the researcher going to define or conceptualize the phenomenon? By now the researcher must have an in-depth understanding of the phenomenon of interest as well as realizing that different researchers have defined and approached this phenomenon in different ways. The framework selected for the study plays an important role in organizing the inquiry as well as many of the components associated to the research process, such as the methods and discussion. Too often individuals struggle making sense of what exactly the framework provides, how it becomes reflected in the study (Grant & Osanloo, 2014), and whether to use a theoretical framework, a conceptual framework, or both (Kivunja, 2018). Most research methods textbooks do not invest time in addressing this opaque issue, and are often insufficiently addressed in research methods courses in higher education curricula, which contributes to the perpetuation of this lack of understanding. Let us invest time clarifying these frameworks. This section assumes researchers know what a *theory* is.

Imagine that the phenomenon of study is the progression of learning mathematical concepts by elementary-age children from households with two parents and two or more children versus households with two parents and a single child. While this seems pretty clear, what is not clear is how the researcher will define some of the important constructs involved in this phenomenon. For example, we know that *learning* has been defined differently by different theories (e.g., behaviorist, humanist, constructivist), and consequently each one would posit different requirements to understand this construct. The behaviorists would expect the researcher to focus only on children's observable and operationally defined behaviors. On the other hand, the constructivists may expect the researcher to focus on the social interactions between the student and the more knowledgeable other (MKO) as well as to pay attention to the verbal and non-verbal communicative exchanges that occur between both. In addition, within this phenomenon, the researcher must consider that there is also the need to explore the role that *parenting* plays in the child's learning process. Once again, there are many theories that explain the parenting construct (e.g., parenting style theory, attachment theory, family systems theory) and consequently, the researcher must identify which theory is most appropriate and add it to the framework. The theoretical framework "undergirds your thinking with regards to how you understand and plan to research your topic, as well as the concepts and definitions from that theory [or theories] that are relevant to your topic" (Grant & Osanloo, 2014, p. 13). The framework becomes the detailed description of how these theories have conceptualized and defined the constructs of this phenomenon (i.e., learning, parenting). It is important to say that a seminal study, or more, could become part of the study's theoretical framework if this provides the researcher with innovative ideas on how to approach the study of the phenomenon of interest. In this sense, the theoretical framework informs the research design and it fundamentally provides the researcher with the parameters as to *what* data should be collected and how the data should be analyzed, interpreted, and eventually discussed (Kivunja, 2018).

"It is important to examine your own epistemological beliefs when selecting a theoretical framework" (Grant & Osanloo, 2014, p. 19). The research paradigm provides an understanding of *how* the data should be collected and analyzed, and it should be aligned to the theoretical framework of the study. For example, the positivist-oriented researcher may aim at quantifying children's learning experiences through possibly direct observations via checklists or with questionnaires that have mostly closed-ended questions for the children, their parents, and/or their teachers. Because of this, the behaviorist theory of learning would be a better fit. The interpretivist-oriented researcher, on the other hand, may aim at writing copious descriptions of what occurs in the classroom and conduct long interviews with the teachers, students, and/ or parents. Because of this, the constructivist theory of learning would be a better fit. The same would occur with the theories on parenting. The researcher must remember that these are theories, and all were developed by researchers whose research paradigms guided their scholarly work. Consequently, some of these theories will align well with the researcher's own research paradigm while others will not. In summary, the theoretical framework "aids the researcher in finding an appropriate research approach, analytical tools and procedures for [their] research inquiry" (Adom et al., 2018, p. 438).

The conceptual framework, on the other hand, is custom-made by the researcher. It provides the opportunity to explain "how the research problem would be explored" (Adom et al., 2018, p. 439). This framework reflects an array of "all the concepts and ideas that occupy your mind as you contemplate, plan, implement and conclude your research project" (Kivunja, 2018, p. 47). Atinkoye (as cited in Adom et al., 2018) suggested that a conceptual framework is "mostly used by researchers when existing theories are not applicable or sufficient in creating a firm structure for the study" (p. 439). In some cases, there is absence of theories explaining the phenomenon of interest, or the researcher may opt to use components from multiple theories or models to frame the study to guide its methodology. Because conceptual frameworks may result from a plethora of components, these are oftentimes represented by diagrams to help the reader better understand them.

It is fair to say that there is ample inconsistency regarding when to use each type of framework. Some authors suggest that interpretivist researchers will utilize conceptual frameworks to guide their studies while positivist researchers will use theoretical frameworks (Adham et al., 2018; Maxwell, 2013). Some suggest that researchers should have one or the other, but not both (Jones, 2015), while others believe the conceptual framework is necessary for conceptualizing or planning the study, but not for conducting the actual research (Knight et al. as cited in Berman, 2013). Not surprisingly, some believe a study should include both frameworks (Adom et al., 2018; Berman, 2013; Kivunja, 2018; Nikitina, 2015). In the end, the researcher is in charge and should know what will better support the efforts to provide a guiding framework for the execution of the study. If the researcher is writing a doctoral dissertation, this is one important issue to discuss with the Dissertation Committee chair. Overall, "researchers and students must tactfully incorporate theoretical and/or conceptual framework in their research inquiries to increase their robustness in all its aspects" (Adom et al., 2018, p. 440). In essence, no study should be written without a methodological guiding framework. Textbox 2.6 (Dass, 2020, p. 8) provides a sample of the theoretical framework for a study addressing equitable academic programming in public secondary schools, and figure 2.2 shows the conceptual framework used to guide a study on corporate training instructor online satisfaction.

TEXTBOX 2.6.
Theoretical Framework

Stacey Adams's Equity Theory provides the foundational context for this study. Established in 1963, Adams's Equity Theory was originally intended to serve the business community, creating a type of check and balance system between the input of employee efforts and the output of perceived rewards garnered by the employee as the outcome of the task. Thus, Equity Theory is predicated on ensuring an equitable distribution of employee performance and dedication to the tasks charged to them (Adams, 1963). Furthermore, Equity Theory is based heavily on employee perception—both within an interpersonal context and a production standpoint. Fowler and Brown (2018) demonstrate the four primary areas in which Equity Theory can be applied in the workplace:

    a. people perceive and evaluate their relationships with others based on a comparison of their input into the relationship and outcomes from the relationship as compared to others' input and outcomes;

    b. if the ratio from the input/outcomes and comparison relationships is not equal according to the perception of the individual, they will determine it to be an inequitable relationship;

    c. the more inequity one feels, the more distress one feels as well; and

    d. the more distress, the more they will work to restore equity.

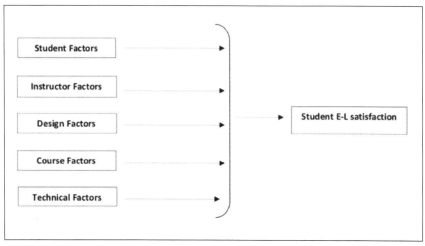

Figure 2.2. Conceptual framework.
Source: Burklund (2020, p. 27).

PURPOSE OF THE STUDY

What exactly will be researched? The reader already knows about the phenomenon of interest by virtue of the previous components (i.e., statement of the problem, theoretical framework). This is the first opportunity to articulate and explicitly state the elements of the study with the purpose of providing "an essential 'road map' to the reader" (Creswell, 1998, p. 96). This statement "follows logically from the identification of the research problem" (Johnson & Christensen, 2017, p. 93) and "enables you to communicate your research project clearly to others" (Johnson & Christensen, 2017, p. 94). It is advisable to start this statement by describing the approach to inquiry (i.e., researcher's paradigm) and proceed by stating the research design, the units of analysis (e.g., single gay women, schools, children's books), and other important variables, concepts, or foci. For example, if this is an autoethnographic study exploring the instructional experiences of teachers working in rural districts and navigating the first few months of the 2020 COVID-19 school closure crisis, then the statement of the problem should link all of those elements: 1) the research method and focus (i.e., autoethnography, journaling instructional experiences), 2) the phenomenon (i.e., COVID-19), and 3) the individuals being impacted by the phenomenon being studied (i.e., school teachers in rural districts facing the school closure crisis). The title of the study should incorporate an abbreviated version of all of these components, as they are the core of the study. Finally, researchers must remember that the purpose statement will also allow the reader to evaluate the innovativeness of the methodological approach as well as its relevance in light of the literature that was presented earlier. Textbox 2.7 (O'Connell, 2020, p. 16) shows the *road map* for a study on the summer slide, and textbox 2.8 (Bremer, 2020, p. 5) presents the road map of a study on the use of rubrics by secondary school teachers.

TEXTBOX 2.7.
Purpose of the Study: Summer Slide

Purpose of the Study

The goal of this mixed-method sequential exploratory study was to create a summer literacy program for middle school students that provided resources typically unavailable in the summer months: transportation, nutrition, and book access. The purpose of this research was to evaluate the effects that result from eliminating barriers to education (e.g., access to educational programs, food insecurity, and book access). The research also assessed the outcomes of the literacy-focused program and variables that motivated participation in the summer learning program.

TEXTBOX 2.8.
Purpose of the Study: Rubrics

Purpose

The purpose of this research project was to look for connections between a secondary teacher's content area the frequency with which they used analytic, holistic, task-specific, and generic rubrics. The research study was descriptive in nature, creating a picture of how teachers used and understood rubrics differently. In analyzing the experiences of secondary language arts, mathematics, science, and social studies teachers, this research could add to the future success of professional development in the area of creating and using rubrics more effectively. This information can also give educators and educational leaders some insight into the ways that teachers think about the nature of knowledge and knowing with regard to their discipline. By asking teachers to define their terms and to share their beliefs about expectations, shared language can be clarified in ways that enhance every teacher's effective use of scoring rubrics. This increases the potential for academic achievement among all students (Whittaker, Salend, & Duhaney, 2001).

RESEARCH QUESTIONS AND HYPOTHESES

What are the driving questions about the phenomenon of interest? Research questions become the central pillar of a given study, and studies are designed with the sole purpose of answering them. The language of the research question informs the methodology to be used. For example, quantitative studies will have research questions that use words such as *effect*, *impact*, and *differences*. On the other hand, within qualitative research, Morse (as cited in Creswell, 1998) indicated that *descriptive* questions were commonly found in ethnographic studies, while *process* and *meaning* questions were more common in grounded theory and phenomenological studies, respectively. There are three important issues to keep in mind when formulating research questions. First, research questions should be open-ended (i.e., avoid yes/no questions). Second, ask *what* and *how* rather than *why* (Creswell, 1998). Third, research questions should be non-directional (Creswell, 1998), that is, researchers should not formulate a question that hints at the expected outcome (e.g., how much faster can native speakers formulate an answer than non-native speakers?). As researchers review the literature, they must pay attention to the research questions and keep note. Making a list will help them learn how to formulate research questions in alignment to the research paradigm as well as the specific methodology used. Table 2.1 shows examples provided by Creswell and Clark (2011, pp. 161–163) of research questions in alignment with the methodology employed. Notice that quantitative research questions and hypotheses clearly communicate the variables that will be measured (i.e., instructional approach, spelling achievement, verbal instructions, rewards, fourth-grade students). In all cases, research questions must be clear and concise.

Table 2.1.   Recommendations for Writing Research Questions.

Qualitative Questions	Quantitative Questions and Hypotheses
What happened? (Central question) Who was involved in response to the incident? (Sub-question) What themes of response emerged during the 8-month period that followed the incident? (Sub-question)	What is the relationship between instructional approach and spelling achievement for fourth-grade students? (Research question) There is no significant difference between the effects of verbal instructions, rewards, and no reinforcement on learning spelling among fourth-grade children. (Null hypothesis) Fourth-grade children performed better on spelling tests when they receive verbal instructions than when they receive rewards or no reinforcement. (Alternative Directional Hypothesis)

Source: Creswell & Clark (2011, pp. 161–163).

Hypotheses are the "predicted outcomes of the study" (Mertler, 2020, p. 11), and are generally found in explanatory or confirmatory quantitative research. As shown in table 2.1, there are two types of hypotheses that are always presented in tandem for a given study: 1) the null hypothesis, which states that there is no observed occurrence (e.g., no impact of the reader's theater strategy on students' reading proficiency levels) and 2) the alternative hypothesis, which states the opposite, that there is an observed occurrence (e.g., there is an impact of the reader's theater on students' reading proficiency levels). Researchers must use inferential statistics to analyze the data and either accept the null hypothesis (i.e., no impact; nothing significant has occurred) or reject the null hypothesis and accept the alternative one (i.e., there is an observed impact and this impact is statistically significant). If the null hypothesis is rejected, then the alternative hypothesis must be accepted providing confirmation that the intervention or treatment resulted in a significant impact as measured on the participants or that differences between groups exist. Exploratory (i.e., descriptive) quantitative research designs and qualitative research designs make no use of hypothesis testing at all; however, they do require the formulation of research questions. Textbox 2.9 (Honetschlager, 2020, pp. 6–7) shows the quantitative research questions guiding the study of a freshman academy program, and textbox 2.10 (Lundberg, 2020, p. 9) shows the research questions guiding a case study (i.e., qualitative methodology). Notice the open-ended nature of these questions.

TEXTBOX 2.9.
Quantitative Research Questions

Primary Research Questions

1. What is the impact of a freshman academy model on student academic achievement, as measured by ninth-grade GPA and credits earned?
2. What is the impact of a freshman academy model on student engagement, as measured by behavior referrals and attendance?
3. What is the impact of a freshman academy on emotional indicators of students' connectedness and positive future outlook, as determined by MN Student Survey?

Secondary Research Questions

4. What are the differences in gender between academic, behavior, and emotional indicators?
5. What are the differences in indicators between students economically disadvantaged (Free or Reduced-Price Lunch) and those classified as not economically disadvantaged in the freshman academy?

TEXTBOX 2.10.
Qualitative Research Questions

Research Questions

1. Which exclusionary discipline disparities exist, and what are their characteristics?
2. What are the practices and educator dispositions in place that cause and perpetuate the disparity?

DEFINITION OF VARIABLES

Each concept, variable, or construct contained in the research questions should be equally understood by the researcher and the readers. In order to achieve that, the researcher needs to ensure that each one of those has a formal definition. Because there are several theoretical definitions associated with the same construct (e.g., learning), the researcher must choose one of them for the study. Which one? Because definitions are associated to theories, the researcher needs to go back to the primary source's theoretical or conceptual framework. For example, the study of the progression of *learning* mathematical concepts by elementary-age children from households with two parents and two or more children versus households with two parents and a single child. If the researcher selected the behaviorist theory to guide the understanding of *learning*, then the researcher should use the behaviorist definition of *learning*.

Each concept, construct, or variable must have a definition retrieved from the literature (i.e., primary or secondary source), and a citation should accompany each one of them. Researchers should stay away from the dictionary and instead focus on theory-based definitions. Because in quantitative research the variables are measured, an *operational* definition must accompany each quantitative variable as well. What this means is that the researcher will need to let the reader know how data collection on each one of these variables will occur. For example, for the variable *learning math,* the researcher could use the summative assessments of a particular grade level as the instruments for data collection. Then, the operational definition for learning math would be the *score* each student obtains on these assessments. The operational definitions should make reference to the specific Appendix entry where the reader can find and inspect the instrument on their own. Oftentimes, demographic variables such as *faculty status* are operationally defined by just one or two items on a given questionnaire. If that was the case, the researcher just needs to make sure those details are clearly spelled out to the reader to ensure clarity and understanding. Also, this level of clarity supports the chances of the study being replicated in the future. Textbox 2.11 (Brekken, 2021, p. 16) presents definitions of variables for a quantitative study on factors supporting or impeding preceptors' willingness to participate in mentorship activities.

TEXTBOX 2.11.
Definition of Variables: Quantitative Design

Variable C: Willingness

Constitutive Definition: The intention to provide mentorship services currently and in the future (Ragins & Scandura, 1999).

Operational Definition: In addition to the online questionnaire development, an online synchronous focus group script was developed. Item number three on the online questionnaire, and item number one on the online synchronous focus group will gather information on willingness to precept. (See items Q3.2.1–Q3.2.11, Q6.9 and 6.12 on Appendix H, and item 1 on Appendix I.)

SIGNIFICANCE OF THE STUDY

Why does this phenomenon need to be researched? In writing this statement about the significance of the study, the researcher needs to think about the "theoretical or practical implications" of conducting it (APA, 2020, p. 76). The narrative must connect the reader back to the gaps and deficiencies of the literature and describe how the study will contribute to filling those gaps or study the phenomenon in methodologically innovative ways. Additionally, the researcher needs to provide a robust argument regarding the impact of the research to the practitioners in this field of study. Back to the *learning math* study, this would mean that the researcher elaborates on the ways practicing teachers would benefit from this study. Lastly, researchers must make sure to elaborate on the potential benefits to the community (e.g., parents, students). Textbox 2.12 (McMahon, 2021, p. 11) shows the significance of the study for a project focused on faculty online instruction.

TEXTBOX 2.12.
Significance of the Study

Significance of the Study

The impact of the quality course design on the student satisfaction and student learning cannot be overstated. Many factors have an impact on the quality of an online course and the preparedness of faculty to create and deliver a quality learning experience is one of those factors (Ali et al., 2005; Meyer & Murrell, 2014; Stupnisky et al., 2018). Faculty experience, professional development choices, and online efficacy beliefs all impact the decisions faculty make that contribute to the design and quality of an online and/or blended course. Determining how the variables in this study are related is important to determine how best to support faculty in providing quality learning experiences for the students they serve.

RESEARCH ETHICS

Research ethics are directly related to the "moral aspects of conducting research" (Mertler, 2020, p. 41). Fundamentally, the researcher needs to ponder what is right or wrong for human subjects participating in research to do or be exposed to as a result of their participation. The central tenet is to ensure that the research methods prevent participants from becoming exposed to any potential source of psychological or physical harm that may jeopardize their welfare or violate their human rights in any way (National Institutes of Health, 2021). Before conducting the study, the researcher must receive training that supports understanding of the procedures involved in protecting human participants' well-being (e.g., consent letter, confidentiality) as well as the procedures required to obtain the Institution Review Board's approval (i.e., IRB approval) or the school, district, corporation, or government approval to carry on this study. All of these requirements apply equally to both qualitative and quantitative research (Creswell & Clark, 2011).

The researcher is in a position of power in regards to the participants (Briggs et al., 2012). Researchers must be cognizant of this, particularly when conducting research with minors or vulnerable populations (e.g., adults with disabilities, undocumented immigrants). The study should describe the strategies in place to ensure all human subjects participating in the study are protected, regardless of their condition or status. The letter giving authorization to conduct the study should be shared with the reader if at all possible (for a thesis or dissertation this is necessary). Otherwise, a statement confirming the date of approval would suffice.

LIMITATIONS AND DELIMITATIONS OF THE STUDY

Limitations of the study will mostly refer to things that are out of the researcher's control. For example, the researcher could be facing low participation because the focus is on a vulnerable population whose members may be fearful of disclosing their status. Another limitation could directly relate to the study's methodology. For example, the instrumentation that will be used in the study may be one of a kind, but not fully vetted for the vulnerable population of interest. The researcher needs to let the reader know that there is awareness of these limitations. This is part of showing transparency and committing to full disclosure as well as serving as a forewarning to future researchers who may become interested in replicating the study.

Delimitations are defined as "chiefly concerned with the scope of the study" (Miles, 2019), which are things that are under the researcher's control (Simon, 2011). For example, a study on undocumented immigrants may focus only on undocumented immigrant women who have children with disabilities. This choice of participants would directly limit the generalizability of the results to all undocumented immigrants. While the researcher could choose to change the inclusion criteria for the study, there is an interest on this specific sub-set of the population, and that is perfectly fine. Simon (2011) recommended explaining the inclusion criteria for the study's participants, the region from where participants were recruited, as well as the professionals or organizations involved or represented. Simon also indicated that stating these are viewed as the most salient delimitations to share with the reader. Again, this is important information to share for the purpose of other researchers replicating the study. Textbox 2.13 (Carlson, 2020, p. 12) shows the limitations on a study regarding novice teachers' teaching effectiveness and textbox 2.14 (Kristjansson-Nelson, 2020, p. 167) shows the delimitations on a study regarding inclusion in media arts education.

TEXTBOX 2.13.
Limitations of the Study

Limitations. The research study was limited to teacher candidates from one mid-size, Midwestern, public, higher education teacher preparation program. Following the year after completion of the teacher prepara-tion program, the CM Transition-to-Teaching Survey is sent to teachers electronically and voluntarily returned. Similarly, the CM Supervisor Sur-vey is emailed to the program completers' supervisor and is voluntarily returned. Previous response rates for the Transition-to-Teaching and Supervisor Survey at the selected institution have been low.

TEXTBOX 2.14.
Delimitations of the Study

As noted, the study was delimited to one non-profit media arts education organization, Bus Stop Films. Thus, an additional delimitation can be found in the range of media arts taught by the organization. Though Bus Stop Films teaches a range of media arts disciplines, including animation and VR, as well as components of all media arts disciplines, film production is by far the primary focus of the organization's curriculum. Thus, the findings are limited to the area of film production and cannot necessarily be general-ized to all media arts disciplines.

CONCLUSION

Once all the components of the Introduction chapter have been de-scribed in great detail in the preceding sections, the researcher needs to wrap up the chapter by providing a summary of what was described. This needs to focus fundamentally on reminding the reader what is the phenomenon being studied as well as the significance of the inquiry. Briefly review the most salient characteristics of the entire chapter (e.g., historical overview, context, gap in the literature). The researcher needs to think about this last paragraph as if this were the abstract of the pre-ceding entire chapter or section. The last sentence or paragraph should provide a preview of what the following chapter will contain.

3

THE LITERATURE REVIEW

PURPOSE OF THE LITERATURE REVIEW

Although the literature review is the second chapter of a traditional dissertation, it is important to understand that the literature review likely starts before one inks the first draft of Chapter 1. Chapter 1, as noted and illustrated in the previous chapter, provides an introduction to the topic, states a purpose of the research (replete with questions and/or hypotheses), establishes definitional parameters, and makes clear the scope of a study. The literature review, although formally beginning once a topic is chosen, tends to begin informally well prior to the moment in which one chooses a topic. There are various components associated with a literature review. These components include content, of which there will be various sub-topics and overall methodological elements involved with one's research.

It is important to understand what is meant by "literature" when conducting a literature review. For purposes of academic writing, including theses, dissertations, and proposals submitted for publication, it is critical to utilize quality sources. Quality sources include seminal works, which will be discussed later in this chapter, but the basic rule is that sources should be peer-reviewed. Peer-reviewed articles are those that have been vetted by experts in the topic area to ensure the research contained in the articles is solid; that is, appropriate methodology, analysis, and findings are valid or trustworthy. Keep in mind the tongue-in-cheek remark, "It must be true because I read it on the Internet" is not true. Make sure that sources are legitimate when including them for purposes of a literature review. The literature review is really a search of literature relevant to one's chosen topic. Briggs et al. (2012) defined a literature search as "a systematic gathering of information relating to a particular topic" (p. 62). The term *systematic* would imply an organized and planned approach to reviewing literature in regard to a specific topic.

The literature review starts in one's mind through the recollection of materials and familiarity with a topic of interest that one has read about and/or experienced in a professional capacity prior to beginning research. As an example, the excerpted parts of the literature review featured in this chapter emerged from an observed need by a practicing superintendent. Although the formal literature review commenced once the study was authorized, the purpose of the study resulted from an observed need and a review of available data and other evidence (e.g., readings and presentations) that made clear the achievement disparities between the White and American Indian populations both in general and in a localized setting prior to any official start of the research project.

A literature review is invaluable for a researcher for multiple reasons. According to Atkinson and Cipriani (2018),

> Literature reviews are conducted for the purpose of (a) locating information on a topic or identifying gaps in the literature for areas of future study, (b) synthesising conclusions in an areas of ambiguity and (c) helping clinicians and researchers inform decision-making and practice guidelines. (p. 74)

The literature review does the following:

- Provides updated information on the current state of the desired research topic. In other words, a search is conducted to find the most recent information regarding a topic, and as a result of recent information, determines if the topic is a worthy undertaking for research.
- Helps to determine whether there are any holes in the available literature that could be filled with the proposed research. Some topics seem saturated, and although it is fine to conduct research

to either corroborate or dispute existing findings, one might find it more valuable to choose a topic that has been less explored or has significant gaps (e.g., when specific populations have never been included in previous research).

- Assists in determining whether the researcher's ideas and beliefs regarding a topic are present in literature, which can help to re-frame one's perspectives by looking at topics in different ways.
- May result in an "aha" moment in which the researcher decides to take the proposed research in a different direction.
- Helps to define both conceptual and theoretical frameworks by ex-amining existing theory and perspectives and noting methodologi-cal approaches used in other studies.

REVIEW OF SOURCES AND LITERATURE REVIEW STRATEGIES

Cognitive Contemplation

Before beginning the formal literature review, which is during the time that one is thinking about the topic of focus, it is important to formulate a plan to review literature. This plan should involve a sys-tematic way to review available literature on a topic, and the review should include seminal sources, when available. When thinking about a topic or sub-topics that are germane to the topic of focus, the task of reviewing literature can seem overwhelming. For example, a Google search of "academic achievement" would yield around 196,000,000 re-sults. While in no way is a simple Google search the preferred or rec-ommended method for conducting a systematic review of literature, it can be utilized as a starting point to foster ideas during the thinking stage. Again, the thinking stage occurs prior to the formal review. This stage allows one to ruminate. Part of the rumination process involves the utilization of current knowledge of a topic combined with new information that is introduced. This new information can come from various sources, but simple Internet searches can help to illuminate topics. With this noted, always keep in mind the source. A general Internet search can provide some insight and ideas, but such action is simply part of an initial discovery period.

Systematic and Narrative Reviews

After the period of cognitive contemplation, which includes one's general knowledge of a topic, general Internet searches, and consideration of other data sources that are readily available, one should determine legitimate avenues to conduct a literature review. There are two types of literature reviews, systematic and narrative, which are mentioned by Atkinson and Cipriani (2018). On one hand, a systematic review of literature is ideal in that it aims to "minimize bias by using explicit, systematic methods documented in advance with a protocol" (Chandler et al., 2019, para. 1). On the other hand, Higgins and Thomas (2019) are clear that systematic reviews must be conducted by a team due to the extensive nature of the time and work associated with these reviews. As a result, research conducted by individuals should involve narrative literature reviews, which are designed to provide a descriptive overview of the literature selected by the researcher, rather than the more comprehensive approach associated with a systematic review. It should be made clear that a narrative review, which is appropriate for individual research projects (e.g., theses, dissertations, and manuscripts) is not inferior to a systematic review of literature. Simply put, the approaches are different, and circumstances will dictate which review would be the most appropriate.

Whereas a narrative literature review describes and discusses the state of a specific topic from a theoretical or contextual point of view, the systematic literature review utilizes a stated methodology to identify, select, and critically evaluate results of studies found in the literature review. A systematic review attempts to collect all the empirical evidence that fits pre-specified eligibility criteria in order to answer a specific research question. It uses clear, systematic methods with a lens to minimize bias in an effort to produce more reliable findings from which conclusions can be drawn and decisions made (Antman et al., 1992; Oxman & Guyatt, 1993).

Bias Avoidance

When conducting a literature review, researchers must guard against bias to the extent possible. Beginning researchers, in particular, tend to want to prove a particular perspective or belief. As a result, a narrative literature review, which involves literature selected by the researchers, can tilt in one direction since the researchers may avoid both published and unpublished research that is contrary to their belief. In the *Prelimi-nary Report: Comprehensive Study of Education and Related Services on the White Earth Indian Reservation* (Bradbury et al., 2010, pp. 30–33), Bradbury could have avoided research that suggested assimilation was a possible solution to the educational and socioeconomic disparities experienced by indigenous populations within the Cultural Factors section of his literature review. Assimilation is viewed as antithetical to cultural pluralism, which is viewed as necessary for systemic change, and the author could have avoided any studies with findings that supported it if he wanted to promote cultural pluralism vis-à-vis systemic change as the best way forward for indigenous populations rather than reporting findings of the benefit of assimilation, which is associated with a hegemonic point of view. However, if Bradbury et al. had avoided contrary viewpoints just to satisfy his own belief system or to meet a particular agenda, then they would have been guilty of bias in reviewing available literature on the topic. The content in textbox 3.1 is taken directly from the work of Bradbury et al., and it illustrates the aforementioned discussion regarding bias in reviewing literature.

TEXTBOX 3.1.

Cultural Factors from the Preliminary Report: Comprehensive Study of Education and Related Services on the White Earth Indian Reservation.

Cultural Factors

Many American Indian children fail to succeed because of issues tied to culture. Swisher (1991) noted that American Indian children often hide academic competence to avoid seeming superior. She explained that in many Native societies, the humility of the individual is a position to be respected and preserved. Advancing oneself above others or taking oneself too seriously violates this key value. If Native children learn best cooperatively, they will experience discomfort and conflicts in classrooms that are too competitive or in which the competition is unfair. Brescia and Fortune (1988) concurred and noted that some tribes may bar competitive behaviors in an academic setting. Florey and Tafoya (1988) seemed to agree by noting American Indian values encourage interdependence,

collective decision-making, and group cohesiveness. Ogbu (1990) explained this attitude among involuntary minorities (e.g., American Indians)
as a folk theory by noting,

> In their folk theories of getting ahead, America's involuntary minorities often
> express the desire to succeed through education just like White Americans.
> However, because many generations of them have faced barriers to the
> opportunity structure as well as severe employment ceilings American invol-
> untary minorities have come to believe that more than education, individual
> effort, and hard work are required for them to overcome those obstacles.
> Consequently, the involuntary minorities' folk theories of how to get ahead
> differ in some significant ways from White middle-class American folk theory
> as well as from that of immigrant minorities. For example, involuntary minor-
> ities stress collective effort as the best means of achieving upward mobility.
> Since America's involuntary minorities do not really believe that the societal
> rules for self-advancement work for them as they do for White Americans,
> their folk theories exhort them to try to change the rules. Thus, rather
> than accept inferior educational standards and facilities or inequitable job
> conditions, American involuntary minorities may try to affect changes in the
> criteria for school credentialing and for employment. This stands in marked
> contrast to that of immigrant minorities, who emphasize following the rules
> of the dominant culture. (p. 49)

Unlike voluntary minorities, who are willing to follow the rules of
dominant culture and view cultural differences as barriers to be overcome,
involuntary minorities see differences as markers of group identity to be
maintained. Ogbu (1990) explained,

> Cultural and language differences become boundary-maintaining mechanisms
> between themselves and the dominant group. Unlike members of immigrant
> groups, America's involuntary minorities, perhaps unconsciously, may per-
> ceive learning or speaking Standard English and practicing other aspects of
> White middle-class culture as threatening to their own minority cultures, lan-
> guages, and identities. Consequently, those members of involuntary minority
> groups who try to cross cultural boundaries may experience social or psy-
> chological pressures from other members of their group not to do so. (p. 48)

If Ogbu's (1990) theory is correct, nothing short of systemic educational change would be needed to significantly increase student achievement among the American Indian population since a buy into the dominant

culture's system would not happen. Ogbu (1990) believed that the relational factor that promotes school success among immigrant minorities involves their degree of acquiescence and trust in the schools and school personnel (p. 52). American Indians tend to distrust institutions that have been established by and are controlled by Caucasians. Ogbu explained,

> The relationship between involuntary minorities and the public schools (and, subsequently, those who control the schools) does not help to promote academic success among involuntary minorities. Generally, involuntary minorities have acquired a basic distrust for the public schools and for school personnel, and they believe that they are provided inferior education for no other reason than because they belong to involuntary minority groups. (p. 54)

The bottom line is that many experts believe that substantial school reform would be needed in order to create the necessary conditions to reduce the achievement gap between American Indian and Caucasian children. Beaulieu (2000) noted,

> With a strong belief that all students can learn, the most basic underlying assumption of school reform is the view that schools as organizations can, in fact, be transformed and improved and that this improvement would result in increased levels of student achievement for all learners. This assumption is based on a certain level of stability and continuity with regard to student enrollment and professional staffing during the school year and succeeding school years. It would also require the existence and availability of a corpus of appropriate information and knowledge to guide professional development as well as curriculum development activities. However, schools with predominantly Indian student populations experience, in fact, extremely high student and staff mobility. These schools also tend to serve student populations disproportionately affected by violence and substance abuse that negatively impact school readiness and individual capacity to learn. These problems are also compounded by the fact that schools serving Native students usually lack the appropriate knowledge base for accomplishing the professional development and curricular development objectives necessary for sustained improvement while also meeting unique social linguistic and cultural needs. (p. 30)

Although systemic change seems necessary in order to accommodate unique cultural features and needs of the American Indian population, some research indicates that assimilation would be a better choice for the American Indian population. Leveque (1994) conducted qualitative research with a fully assimilated American Indian population in California. Leveque suggested:

> The first variable, the change from caste-like to immigrant status via choice, suggests that Ogbu's categories of immigrant and non-immigrant minorities are not static: caste-like minorities in the U.S. may not be bound to their caste-like status. The key element for Native Americans in Barstow was choice. This group chose to leave their reservations and to live in the majority society. They have thus become immigrants by Ogbu's definition. Immigrant minorities usually assimilate by the third generation; these Native Americans had assimilated by the third generation. (p. 30)

Apparently, the assimilation yielded great educational dividends and the study has set the table for future studies that would be similar in nature. Leveque (1994) noted:

> This single case study opens questions for further study. The findings have indicated that a small group of Native Americans who came to Barstow from three major tribal reservations located in the Southwestern U.S. have assimilated into the majority culture within three generations. As a result, the grandchildren and great-grandchildren of these immigrants have exhibited academic achievement levels comparable to those of their peers in the setting. The major reason that assimilation was successful for this group was that they chose a particular way of life in a particular setting. They have chosen to become a part of the majority culture in Barstow. (p. 33)

Leveque's (1994) case study is indeed fascinating in that it raises the question as to whether minorities should forsake cultural identity in order to experience educational and socioeconomic success. Moreover, the study provides an impetus for similar research projects. Leveque (1994) is clearly provocative in noting,

> Several concerns arise as a result of the findings and conclusions of this study. The academic success of the Native students in Barstow was related to the fact that they lived one cultural life: the life of the majority culture. Their Native ways were virtually lost. Must loss of culture be the price paid for academic success for Native Americans or any minority? Replication of this study in other settings, including reservation settings, would further clarify, support, or refute issues raised in this single study. (p. 34)

In reading the portion of the literature review put forth by Bradbury (Bradbury et al., 2010), it should be evident that he tried to present findings that supported both sides of the assimilation/cultural pluralism discussion. While understanding fully that a narrative review of literature is a descriptive overview of the literature selected by the researcher, this does not excuse the researcher from including relevant literature that fails to support the researcher's hypothesis or general point of view.

Seminal Works

The term *seminal* may be unfamiliar to beginning researchers. When used within the context of published materials, seminal works are those that are viewed as critical or key studies, books, or legal decisions that have left an indelible mark on a particular topic. Whether conducting a systematic or narrative literature review, the researcher would be remiss if seminal works germane to the topic were not included. Seminal works are those that have left a strong imprint on the way scholars think about and approach particular topics, policy decisions, and even matters of legality. Northcentral University Library (2020) defined seminal works as follows:

> Seminal works, sometimes called pivotal or landmark studies, are articles that initially presented an idea of great importance or influence within a particular discipline. Seminal articles are referred to time and time again in the research, so you are likely to see these sources frequently cited in other journal articles, books, dissertations, etc.
>
> Identifying seminal articles relies heavily on your own thoroughness in the examination and synthesis of the scholarly literature. Typically, there will not be any explicit labels placed on articles, identifying them as seminal. Rather, you will begin to see the same authors or articles cited frequently. *It is important to keep in mind that seminal studies may have been published quite some time ago. Limiting a database search to only the past 5 years, for example, may exclude seminal studies from your results.* To avoid overlooking pivotal research that may have occurred in years past, it is recommend that you do *not* use a date limiter. (paras. 1–2)

Bradbury (Bradbury et al., 2010) included seminal works within his literature review. For example, as noted in the previous section of this chapter, Bradbury utilized both paraphrasing and direct quotes from the works of Ogbu (1990). According to Carter (2004),

> For several decades, the late educational scholar John U. Ogbu theorized about and studied the academic performance of immigrant and non-immigrant (also referred to as voluntary and involuntary, respectively) minority students. Although often contested in the field of education for overgeneralizations regarding the academic performance of these students, Ogbu's work has been seminal in understanding the attitudes and behaviors of Black students in public schools. (para. 4)

Although Ogbu's works focus particularly on Black students, both Blacks and American Indians are viewed as involuntary minorities. As a result, Ogbu's seminal works are relevant to a literature review focused on the academic success of American Indian students.

Another example of the inclusion of a seminal work in Bradbury's (Bradbury et al., 2010) study is Jon Reyhner. As noted in the North-central University Library (2020, para. 2) definition of seminal works, "Typically, there will not be any explicit labels placed on articles, identifying them as seminal. Rather, you will begin to see the same authors or articles cited frequently." Jon Reyhner is a name that surfaces a great deal within research regarding academic achievement and equity issues involving indigenous populations. A review of his biographical sketch would make clear why this is given his extensive history and involvement with scholarship associated with indigenous populations (Northern Arizona University, 2020). Bradbury (Bradbury et al., 2010) utilized two sources authored by Reyhner (1992, 1993):

> Reyhner (1992) believed that Native students are denied a curriculum that includes their heritage and culturally biased tests are used to label them as failures and push them out of academic programs. Rather than dropouts failing the system, the traditional school system has failed the dropouts. Reyhner (1992) saw the idea that Native Americans are culturally disadvantaged or culturally deprived as an ethnocentric bias that should not be continued. (Bradbury et al., 2010, pp. 33–34)

> Reyhner (1993) noted that teacher education programs for teachers of Native children should integrate information on Native educational history and philosophies into foundations classes, integrate research findings

of successful minority education programs into methods classes, introduce pre-service teachers to the wide variety of Native education materials, and provide field experiences with Native students in exemplary schools. (Bradbury et al., 2010, p. 34)

It should be noted that Jon Reyhner is as relevant in 2021 as he was in 1992 given his substantial contributions for decades to the topic of indigenous education. As noted previously by Northcentral University Library (2020), using a date limiter in a search would have excluded these important works.

Other Works

Within a literature review, most cited works will not be seminal. This does not mean that these works are unimportant. Simply put, the status of *seminal works* is reserved for those works that have left an indelible influence on a particular topic or theme. In regard to other works, two questions often surface. First, how old is too old for a reference? Second, is there a number of works that should be cited for a particular academic pursuit (e.g., dissertation)?

In tackling the question of whether a source is dated, one must consider whether the information would still be relevant. Take, for example, the topic of distance education. An article from the late 20th century may not be relevant if one considers the changes that have occurred with distance education between the 1990s and 2022. On the other hand, an article containing certain best pedagogical practices (e.g., relationship building) from the 1990s may still be relevant in 2022. When employing a narrative literature review, the researcher must make judgment calls as to whether older articles are still relevant.

In regard to the number of sources needed for a particular paper (e.g., journal article), there is no clear answer. One hundred sources aren't necessarily superior to 50 sources. A basic principle is whether the sources in aggregate have allowed the researcher to canvass the chosen topic within the scope of the research project. The researcher should utilize multiple sources to corroborate major themes within the literature review, while at the same time providing any divergent findings or viewpoints that may be present. When in doubt, the researcher should err on the side of more sources than fewer.

Annotated Bibliography

Whether a full-fledged doctoral student or a practitioner with interest in a particular topic, a solid literature review practice involves an annotated bibliography. However, by definition, an annotated bibliography has two parts, a citation in the required style format and an annotation. According to Purdue Online Writing Lab (n.d.), an annotation should be several sentences that summarize the main point of the reviewed article, and it should contain one's own assessment of the value of the article in relation to one's chosen topic. The compilation of an annotated bibliography can start prior to the commencement of research. As a professional, the ongoing creation of an annotated bibliography can provide an invaluable resource and guide to help recall particular articles for both practitioner and scholarship reference. Good examples of sources that contain both an annotation and evaluation of usefulness follow:

Bahn, S. (2011). Community safety and recidivism in Australia: Breaking the cycle of reoffending to produce safer communities through vocational training. *International Journal of Training Research, 9*(3), 261–266.
　　This article explores the use of vocational training as a mechanism of effective community reintegration. Done in Australia, this research advocates for a linkage between in-prison education and support services post release. This article is valuable to my research because it clearly displays how vocational education can be the foundation of successful community reintegration.

Kantor, H. (1991, Nov). Education, social reform, and the state: ESEA and federal education policy in the 1960s. *American Journal of Education, 100*(1), 47–83. Retrieved from https://www.jstor.org/stable/1085652?readnow=1&seq=1#metadata_info_tab_contents.
　　Kantor discusses rationales and political terrain on the War on Poverty, the making of the Great Society, and President Johnson's authorization of ESEA. Both sides (for and against) the ESEA and War on Poverty are discussed. Kantor described the culture of poverty thesis and how it was a driving force behind the Act. Kantor describes how politicians knew they could not directly create laws to impact public education, but could use the power of taxation and offering of financial support (or lack thereof) to influence education. This article is comprehensive and offers quotes and details that may be helpful for a brief on this time in history.

An annotated bibliography is invaluable for the rigorous researcher since it contains a summary of the relevant articles and specific information as to why articles are valuable. Since annotated bibliographies become large over time, it is recommended that the researcher find ways to code (e.g., color, numerical) in such a way so as to know which articles pertain to a particular part of one's topic. For example, if one compares the Reyhner (1992, 1993) articles used by Bradbury (Bradbury et al., 2010) in the Seminal Works section of this chapter, it becomes apparent that the two sources, while authored by the same person, pertain to different aspects of indigenous education. One article (Reyhner, 1992) focused on indigenous education (e.g., curriculum, dropouts, and bias) within the P–12 system whereas the other article (Reyhner, 1993) focused on teacher education programs regarding indigenous populations. While both topics are relevant to Bradbury's work, they examine different items associated with indigenous education. As a result, it would be important to have these sources coded in some way so as to facilitate the writing of the literature review. If, for example, Reyhner (1992) were coded in blue and Reyner (1993) were coded in yellow, one could expect upon completion of the literature search that several other sources would be coded in blue and yellow. Once sources are grouped, the synthesis of literature becomes far easier.

Sources and Legitimate Search Avenues

When conducting a literature review, the origin of sources matters. Wikipedia can be a general starting point to establish general information regarding a topic, but it is not considered an acceptable source of scholarship work. Instead, peer-reviewed literature (e.g., journals, books, theses, and dissertations) should be used. Although the quality or relevancy of journal articles and books can vary, the stamp of "peer-reviewed" helps to ensure that the reported research is sound.

There are various ways to find reputable sources for purposes of a literature review. Internet searches can produce helpful and reputable publications, but one would need to sift through a lot of possibilities to find useful items. If utilizing the Internet to search, Google Scholar is a good choice. Simply type "Google Scholar" in a browser, and there is an option to search articles, case law, book reviews, technical reports, and more. Both topics and authors can be entered into the Google Scholar search. Upon entering "Boyd Bradbury," for example, who is a co-author of this book, a list of published works would appear. The following examples are provided to give the researcher a sense of the manner in which Google Scholar displays available works. In most cases, the desired article or book chapter can be downloaded immediately.

[PDF] Fundamentals of New Effective System to Accelerate Language Acquisition Using Visual Approach
BL Bradbury, IH Tahini, AK Dadykin—2018—ijiet.org
   Increased migration of individuals from one country to another poses the challenge of accelerating improved language acquisition while reducing the cost of language training. This work strives to find new ways to improve communication and understanding, including . . .
Cited by 10 Related articles All 3 versions

[PDF] researchgate.net
[BOOK] A qualitative study of the factors related to the academic success of American Indian students
BL Bradbury—2005—researchgate.net
   A substantial academic achievement disparity exists nationally between American Indian and Caucasian populations. This disparity is evident at Waubun-Ogema-White Earth Community Schools (WOWE), which is a public school district that is located on the White . . .
Cited by 3 Related articles All 6 versions

[PDF] researchgate.net
[BOOK] Authority and leadership via a multiple frames approach
BL Bradbury, KV Halbur, DA Halbur—2010—books.google.com
   The only aspect of education that is truly static is its propensity to change. As such, leaders have both the capacity and the responsibility to respond to change. In educational settings, leaders are frequently facing issues such as shrinking budgets, restructuring, and . . .
Cited by 6 Related articles All 3 versions

In these examples, one can see that articles are available through ResearchGate (www.researchgate.com), which is a large academic social network for researchers. Although researchers must be registered to upload scholarly articles, books, and projects, users do not need membership to access the available resources. However, since registration is free and easy, one can get full access to the benefits of ResearchGate through registration. Many scholarly articles via ResearchGate are reputable, but one caveat is that articles can be uploaded to ResearchGate without quality assurances of peer review. As a result, one should make certain that any articles utilized from ResearchGate are peer-reviewed and published in reputable journals or other credible venues. With this noted, however, there are many credible and reputable publications on ResearchGate. For example, John Creswell, who is considered the preeminent source on mixed methods research, qualitative research, and research design, has published works on ResearchGate, and he participates in ResearchGate discussion forms with regularity. An added benefit to ResearchGate involves question and answer threads regarding various topics. Registration with ResearchGate is required to participate in the threads, but access to the threads for purposes of reading does not require registration. For example, one researcher had a question on conceptual framework, which generated many responses (Otto, 2019). These responses provide both general guidance and additional resources. The original question and excerpt follow.

Martin Ott, Solomon Islands National University, asked the following question on October 4, 2019: How to build a conceptual framework in qualitative research? I am working on my proposal for my study that is qualitative. As a novice researcher I am trying to understand how I should build my conceptual framework as part of my proposal. I have read responses to questions raised on the same question and some responses seem to be helping. The other day I was watching a YouTube on the topic and it listed three elements that make up conceptual framework. The present listed:

1. Personal interest
2. Topical research
3. Theoretical framework

This confuses me; however, I took as the framework should capture the three. I need help.

Boyd Bradbury added an answer, October 10, 2019: As some-one who oversees a doctoral program, I get a lot of questions regarding conceptual versus theoretical frameworks. Some researchers use these terms interchangeably, but they are different. Let me try to put this distinction in simple words. A conceptual framework is really a plan. What is the issue that you want to address, and what would be a reasonable approach to shed some light on the issue? The conceptual framework allows you to have a basic plan or map to follow your efforts to answer your questions. Literature reviews can help you to gather a conceptual framework in that you will start to see potential approaches and major themes/findings that help you to see established connections, or at least related ones, between your desired focus and what has been discovered previously. A theoretical framework is a bit different in that it gets at your actual research paradigm with greater specificity. Are you going to subscribe to constructivism or take a critical approach? This will determine your perspective when approaching research. Perhaps you will utilize a feminist perspective or a pragmatic (e.g., Dewey) approach? The approach will drive your methodology, to an extent. You will need to determine whether ethnography, action research, grounded theory, or something else would serve as the best methodological approach. In addition, you will need to determine methods/tools to collect data. Will you opt to utilize surveys to capture perception phenomena, focus groups, interviews, or would narrative inquiry best help to answer the research question?

Bahram Shahedi added an answer, October 16, 2019: Doing a proposal on a qualitative research does not mean you are off the hook of theories. Try to develop or conceptual framework as a general under-standing of a thought, event, process, and a course of action to guide your research by emerging key statements and concepts out of your exploratory review of literature and theoretical foundation.

Ndalahwa MUSA Masanja added an answer, December 22, 2019: Qualitative research's conceptual framework can be developed based on your research problem, objective, and question(s). The goal of the conceptual framework is to illustrate your research approach in some pictorial and text forms to ease readers' understanding of your research approach.

Refer to the resources links provided below about the conceptual framework for a qualitative research.

http://www.sagepub.com/sites/default/files/ump-binaries/48247
  _ch3_.pdf
http://journals.rcni.com/doi/pdfplus/10/7748/nr.21.6.34.e1252
http://fsg.afre.msu.edu/sambia/Conceptual_Framework_and_Re
  search_Questions.pdf

Sammy Azer added an answer, January 13, 2020: Martin Otto— thank you for your interesting question. Building a conceptual framework and supporting results through theoretical frames aim at strengthening the discussion, explaining and making predictions. Linking the work with theory enables a set of interrelated propositions or concepts in defining points raised and connecting the findings into a meaningful phenomenon. I recommend reading the work of Smith Mj and Liehr P 1999, published in *Research and Theory for Nursing Practice*.

✿   ✿   ✿

Another approach to literature searches involves database utilization at college and university libraries. Access to expensive databases is one of the perks of being a student, and the bottom line is that students are paying for this access, albeit indirectly. As a result, the lack of database utilization renders it an untapped resource. At Minnesota State University Moorhead (MSUM), the institution of higher education at which the co-authors of this book are employed, access to library databases is obtained through Livingston Lord Library (https://libguides.mnstate .edu/az.php). At MSUM, researchers (students and faculty members) have access to popular databases, such as Academic Search Complete, Education Research Complete (Ebsco), and ERIC. These databases contain recent publications, and reference librarians are available to assist students with search processes and terms that are most likely to yield results. At many institutions of higher education, including MSUM, these databases can be accessed virtually. Moreover, at MSUM and many institutions of higher education, interlibrary loan is available. Interlibrary loan allows both email downloads of articles and physical copies of books delivered to an address of choice.

Topical Outline

It is important to keep in mind that the literature review is both planned and organized. As a result, one can either create a topical outline prior to the literature review or after reviewing literature. If the former approach were taken, it is likely that the researcher would have a solid sense of available literature on the topic before starting the review. If the latter approach were taken, the topical outline would be developed after a review of enough sources to get reasonable depth and breadth of a topic. In both cases, the topical outline may continue to evolve as more sources are reviewed.

An example of a topical outline, which is representative of literature searched for a dissertation study (Bradbury, 2005) and subsequent White Earth studies (Bradbury et al., 2010; Bradbury et al., 2012) featured in this book, can be found in textbox 3.2. The *Comprehensive Study of Education and Related Services on the White Earth Indian Reservation* (Bradbury et al., 2012) occurred in two parts. The first part (Phase I) of this study utilized existing data to establish the current state of educational programming and related services for children attending nine school districts on or near the White Earth Indian Reservation, and matters related to health care, social services, early childhood education, postsecondary education, and justice. The second part (Phase II) of this study is comprised of several parts: 1) early childhood education; 2) education in Grades 3–12; 3) social services; and 4) health services with the purpose of determining findings and recommendations to address the issue of achievement associated with the American Indian child living on or near the White Earth Indian Reservation.

TEXTBOX 3.2.
White Earth Study Topical Outline

Thesis/Hypothesis/Research Outcome: The issue of underachievement of American Indian children living on or near the White Earth Indian Reservation is both verifiable and complicated. While data confirm the existence of educational disparity between American Indian children and their Caucasian counterparts, the establishment of underlying causes and the prescription of remedies prove challenging.

Topical Outline: Comprehensive Study of Education and Related Services on the White Earth Indian Reservation

I. Introduction
  A. Brief Historical Context
    1. Involuntary Minorities
    2. U.S. Government Actions
      a. Military Action
      b. Reservations
      c. Assimilation
      d. Self-determination/Sovereignty
  B. American Indians: U.S. Demographics
    1. Historical Demographics
    2. Current Demographics
      a. Overall Percentage of U.S. Population
      b. Salient Demographic Features of American Indian Population
  C. American Indians and Education
    1. Historical Context
      a. Assimilationist Policies and Practices
      b. Boarding Schools
      c. Self-determination
    2. Modern Concerns
      a. Cultural Pluralism
      b. Multicultural Education
      c. Cultural Competence

II. Achievement Disparity
  A. Nationally
  B. White Earth Reservation

III. Non-Education Matters Related to American Indian Achievement
  A. Poverty
  B. Sanitation
  C. Health Disparities
  D. Cultural Factors
  E. Historical Trauma

IV. Educational Matters Related to American Indian Achievement
  A. Testing
  B. Curriculum
  C. Teaching Methods/Approaches
  D. Teacher Education/Preparation
  E. Professional Development

V. Conclusion
  A. Summary of Major Points
  B. Discussion

Literature Review Analysis and Synthesis

Although a topical outline helps to guide the literature search and an annotated bibliography helps to determine the content and usefulness of sources, the literature review needs to result in more than a compilation of resources. Instead, the literature review requires higher levels of Bloom's Taxonomy (Armstrong, n.d.); those are analysis and synthesis. The following two examples, the correct one excerpted from Bradbury et al. (2010, p. 30) and a created incorrect one, are designed to convey both the correct and incorrect ways to write a literature review. In particular, these examples focus on words that help dovetail or feather the literature review for purposes of showing corroboration or divergent findings. These words are found in italics. A well-written literature review should result in the synthesis of sources rather than the stacking of one thought onto another.

Correct Example

Many American Indian children fail to succeed because of issues tied to culture. Swisher (1991) noted that American Indian children often hide academic competence to avoid seeming superior. She explained that in many Native societies, the humility of the individual is a position to be respected and preserved. Advancing oneself above others or taking oneself too seriously violates this key value. If Native children learn best cooperatively, they will experience discomfort and conflicts in classrooms that are too competitive or in which the competition is unfair. Brescia and Fortune (1988) *concurred* and noted that some tribes may bar competitive behaviors in an academic setting. Florey and Tafoya (1988) *seemed to agree* by noting American Indian values encourage interdependence, collective decision-making, and group cohesiveness. Ogbu (1990) *explained* this attitude among involuntary minorities (e.g., American Indians) as a folk theory.

> In their folk theories of getting ahead, America's involuntary minorities often express the desire to succeed through education just like White Americans. However, because many generations of them have faced barriers to the opportunity structure as well as severe employment ceilings American involuntary minorities have come to believe that more

than education, individual effort, and hard work are required for them to overcome those obstacles. Consequently, the involuntary minorities' folk theories of how to get ahead differ in some significant ways from White middle-class American folk theory as well as from that of immigrant minorities. For example, involuntary minorities stress collective effort as the best means of achieving upward mobility. Since America's involuntary minorities do not really believe that the societal rules for self-advancement work for them as they do for White Americans, their folk theories exhort them to try to change the rules. Thus, rather than accept inferior educational standards and facilities or inequitable job conditions, American involuntary minorities may try to affect changes in the criteria for school credentialing and for employment. This stands in marked contrast to that of immigrant minorities, who emphasize following the rules of the dominant culture. (p. 49)

Incorrect Example

Many American Indian children fail to succeed because of issues tied to culture. Swisher (1991) noted that American Indian children often hide academic competence to avoid seeming superior. She explained that in many Native societies, the humility of the individual is a position to be respected and preserved. Advancing oneself above others or taking oneself too seriously violates this key value. If Native children learn best cooperatively, they will experience discomfort and conflicts in classrooms that are too competitive or in which the competition is unfair. Brescia and Fortune (1988) found that some tribes may bar competitive behaviors in an academic setting. Florey and Tafoya (1988) reported that American Indian values encourage interdependence, collective decision-making, and group cohesiveness. Ogbu (1990) put forth a folk theory.

> In their folk theories of getting ahead, America's involuntary minorities often express the desire to succeed through education just like White Americans. However, because many generations of them have faced barriers to the opportunity structure as well as severe employment ceilings American involuntary minorities have come to believe that more than education, individual effort, and hard work are required for them to overcome those obstacles. Consequently, the involuntary minorities' folk theories of how to get ahead differ in some significant ways from White

middle-class American folk theory as well as from that of immigrant minorities. For example, involuntary minorities stress collective effort as the
best means of achieving upward mobility. Since America's involuntary minorities do not really believe that the societal rules for self-advancement
work for them as they do for White Americans, their folk theories exhort
them to try to change the rules. Thus, rather than accept inferior educational standards and facilities or inequitable job conditions, American
involuntary minorities may try to affect changes in the criteria for school
credentialing and for employment. This stands in marked contrast to that
of immigrant minorities, who emphasize following the rules of the dominant culture. (p. 49)

In the aforementioned examples, one can see the difference between
an analyzed and synthesized literature review through connection
among articles in the correct example as opposed to a simple reporting
of what a source said without tying the information to other examples.
In the correct example, words such as *concurred, seemed to agree,* and
explained this attitude (with reference to the other sources) synthesize
the articles in an intelligible way. Prior to synthesis, however, one must
analyze sources for purposes of corroboration or disparate findings.

One should keep in mind that a topical outline can be used to help
organize sources so as to facilitate synthesized writing in a logical and
fluid way. As mentioned previously, coding (e.g., color) of some sort can
help with this process. For example, under *Non-Education Matters Related to American Indian Achievement* (see table 3.4), *Poverty* is listed
as a sub-topic. By following the topical outline and using sources coded
under *Poverty*, it would be far easier to synthesize available literature
on testing by utilizing words such as *agreed, concurred,* and *disagreed.*
Moreover, additional explanation can occur when linking agreement
or disagreement from sources. In Bradbury et al. (2010), this synthesis
is evident through words such as *agreed,* and additional explanation is
provided to illuminate the impact of poverty,

Although the poverty outlook for American Indians is dismal, statistics
for those living on reservations or trust lands is even worse. Antell et al.
(1999) noted that compared to non-reservation American Indians, income
for American Indians living on reservations drops by approximately half
and poverty levels increase appreciably, to about 51% of all American Indian households. Save the Children (2002) agreed and noted that Ameri-

can Indian reservations are pockets of poverty where the child poverty
rate is two to three times the national average and where families have
been locked in a cycle of poverty for decades. In all likelihood, the lack of
employment opportunities on reservations leads to the out-migration of
the most talented and better educated American Indians, which exacer-
bates the already exceptionally high unemployment rates and low incomes
among American Indians who live on reservations. (pp. 24–25)

Another way in which one can demonstrate agreement and synthesis
of sources involves the utilization of multiple citations after one source.
For example, Bradbury (2010) could have provided the state of poverty
related to American Indians in an alternative format as follows:

The poverty outlook for American Indians is dismal. Poverty impacts a
majority of American Indian households, and poverty impacts American
Indian children at a disproportionate rate. The poverty rate is amplified
for American Indians who reside on reservations. (Antell et al., 1999; Save
the Children, 2002)

Helpful Tips

One caveat associated with literature reviews is that there must be an
end to reviewing literature. While it might be tempting to continue to
review articles and books, one can lose valuable time going down what is
referred to as "rabbit holes." Although some rabbit holes prove enlight-
ening, an inability to wrap up the literature review can result in schedule
delays that could hinder the completion of one's research project on
time. As a researcher, one must determine when enough material (a saturation point) has been reviewed to communicate in a comprehensive
and succinct fashion the necessary context for one's research project.

In communicating available literature on a topic, try to use primary
sources to the extent possible (e.g., research article, technical report).
Many times, one can come upon a primary source that utilizes many
credible secondary sources (e.g., books). As a researcher, it is perfectly
acceptable to retrieve, read, and use those secondary sources. Moreover, one should pay attention to sources that are cited with regularity
throughout the literature search. In all likelihood, these sources should
be included in one's literature review. Keep in mind that not all sources
are of equal value. Even peer-reviewed resources can vary in quality and

rigor. When reviewing sources, keep in mind items such as paradigms, methodological approaches, sample sizes, demographics, and generalizability to provide a balanced search and review of literature in an effort to reduce bias and comprehensiveness to the extent possible. Many times, a particular article produces a reputable reference list. In this case, one would be wise to seek out those reputable articles, read them, and utilize those sources in one's own research, as appropriate.

Although there are basic writing styles (e.g., APA7) that must be followed, the correct style will be communicated by one's program. Moreover, most programs provide dissertation templates, checklists, and associated documents to help guide researchers. If doctoral advisers and instructors do not provide these sorts of documents, the student should ask. Finally, review research projects that have been completed by previous graduates of one's program. It can be quite helpful to get a sense of the specifics and quality of previous research that has been approved.

CONCLUSION

The literature review, which is traditionally the second chapter of a doctoral dissertation and a key aspect of most academic publications, is a search of literature relevant to one's topic and the methodological aspects of one's research. The literature review should occur in an organized and systematic way, and it requires both analysis and synthesis of relevant sources. A literature review is not a basic list of findings that stack one after another without connections. It is a blending of sources to provide a reasonably comprehensive backdrop or context within which one's research would occur. The literature review should highlight both corroborated and disparate findings. The literature review should help one to refine conceptual and theoretical frameworks through an understanding of both findings and research methodologies associated with the chosen topic. Various items, such as an annotated bibliography and a topical outline, are helpful in conducting a successful review of literature.

4

METHODOLOGY

The methodology of a research project is fundamental to assess the adequacy of a researcher's plan to produce a valid understanding of the phenomenon being studied; that is, the methodology provides the necessary elements to judge the robustness of a given research project (Kallet, 2004). Important questions include: Are the procedures aligned to the research question(s)? Are data analyses adequate and sufficient? Do the methodology components make sense in light of the statement of the problem and research questions? Writing the methodology of a proposed study demands from the researcher a high level of systematization that should account for a myriad of components (e.g., instrumentation, hypotheses statements, sampling procedures, sample size calculation, robustness checks) that together produce a study ready to stand up to scrutiny.

"Generalization is the origin of knowledge" (Morales-Bermudez, 2011, p. 250) and the methodology should provide other researchers with a recipe for the replication of the study. The scientific community values these replications as they provide "supporting (or contradicting) evidence regarding the existence of a phenomenon" (Pedersen & Stritch, 2018, p. 606) and consequently strengthen the validity and generalizability of the results. Because of this, the researcher should generate a detailed, chronologically driven, and organized description of all the steps taken in order to execute the study. In that respect, the methodology should provide as much detail as possible (Wiersma, 1995). While much of this rich, detailed information would not get published in a peer-reviewed journal due to space limitations, in a dissertation this is considered best practice. Having said that, the researcher will need to navigate a delicate balance between providing insufficient details and burdening the reader with irrelevant information (American Psychological Association, [APA] 2020). This chapter will help researchers write, step-by-step, the methodology section of the research project. What follows are the sections that should be contained in any *Methods* or *Methodology* section or chapter for a manuscript or a doctoral dissertation, respectively. Each section will include a description of what should be included as well as specific examples to support understanding.

INTRODUCTION

The introduction presents the reader with the focus of the study. The American Psychological Association (APA, 2020) recommends to start by presenting the problem in a succinct but general way (i.e., *statement of the problem*). Next, the researcher must provide "historical antecedents" (p. 76), that is, a brief literature review describing what has been the "scope of the problem, its context, and its theoretical or practical implications" (p. 76). At the end of this historical review, the researcher must articulate what are the current gaps of the literature and describe the concrete ways the study cannot only contribute to fill said gaps but also help move forward the knowledge about this phenomenon. *Phenomenon*, in research, is used as a synonym for *problem* or *focus of the study*. Lastly, the researcher needs to articulate the *purpose of the study* or the study's goals (i.e., what it is that the study will accomplish). These goals will be a little different if the study is quantitative (e.g., research questions), qualitative (e.g., approach to inquiry), or mixed methods.

The introduction should be brief, about two or three paragraphs long, and should be written using sentences that will pick the reader's interest, highlighting on what is unique or distinct about the study (Creswell,

2014). The introduction section should mention again what is the problem, the purpose, and the research questions. These are elements that were described in detail in Chapter 2. Textbox 4.1 (O'Connell, 2020, p. 16) shows the statement of the problem for a study that focused on the *summer slide* phenomenon affecting students' academic achievement. Textbox 4.2 (O'Connell, 2020, p. 16) shows the study's respective *purpose of the study*, while textbox 4.3 (O'Connell, 2020, p. 17) shows the study's *research question.*

TEXTBOX 4.1.
Summer Slide Study: Partial Statement of the Problem

Despite all efforts to improve student learning with summer school, some researchers note that summer school does not reduce the achievement gap. Entwisle et al. (2001) stated that "on average, the summer school gain for students of all socioeconomic levels is quite small" (p. 13). Borman et al. (2005) similarly argued that there are too few high-quality studies on the "potential achievement effects associated with summer school" (p. 135) and few studies that track multi-year summer programs. More research into quality summer learning programs is needed to investigate possible solutions to the summer slide.

TEXTBOX 4.2.
Summer Slide Study: Partial Purpose of the Study

The goal of this mixed-method sequential exploratory study was to create a summer literacy program for middle school students that provided resources typically unavailable in the summer months: transportation, nutrition, and book access. The purpose of this research was to evaluate the effects that result from eliminating barriers to education (e.g., access to educational programs, food insecurity, and book access). The research also assessed the outcomes of a literacy-focused program and variables that motivated participation in the summer learning program.

The researcher must notice how all of these descriptions are aligned; they allude to the same variables (i.e., summer slide, students' achievement); additionally, attention should be given to the primary research question as it contains the elements that will guide the methodology of the study. Specifically, the research questions should hint at the research design as well as the potential data analyses required to bring meaning to the problem being studied (both will be described later in this chapter). For example, if the research question uses terms such as *impact* or *effect*, then the reader will know that a comparison of groups will take place and that the researcher will measure the impact or effect of a treatment used in the study via a MANOVA, t-Test, or any other inferential statistic used with the purpose of comparing means. For instance, the mean literacy test score from a group of immigrant students from Somalia, before and after the implementation of the repeated reading instructional strategy.

Textbox 4.3 contains three research questions. The first research question is the one addressing the overall problem, which is the impact that summer vacations had on students' academic performance (i.e., *summer slide*). The researcher was interested in literacy performance in particular. The other research questions addressed specific components of the treatment (i.e., literacy summer program) that were designed to counter the effects of the summer slide.

TEXTBOX 4.3.

Summer Slide Study: Research Questions

1. How does a literacy-focused summer program affect students' reading outcomes?
2. How do student and family incentives affect summer school registration and attendance?
3. How do school-provided summer learning opportunities (book distribution and a literacy-based summer program) affect motivation to read for middle school readers?

In closing, the introduction should captivate the audience's interest by conveying the researcher's research vision. Consequently, the researcher must capitalize on this opportunity to create the right platform for the research idea. After all, this research idea is relevant and significant to the researcher as a professional, to the community from where participants will be recruited, and is expected to contribute to the theoretical and practical growth of this field of studies.

RESEARCH DESIGN

Unless the researcher has been engaged in research and knows which design is needed for the study, there is a need to explore a few issues first. This process starts with the identification of the *research paradigm.* That is, when asked about reality, what is it that the researcher believes in? What are the necessary elements needed to have in place when confronted with the question, "What is real and how can this be demonstrated?" The research paradigm determines how a phenomenon should be studied as well as how the data should be collected and interpreted to bring comprehensive meaning to the phenomenon (Kivunja & Kuyini, 2017). The research paradigm is a set of common beliefs and agreements shared between scientists about how problems should be understood and addressed (Kuhn, 1962). It is clear that the paradigm is a powerful lens through which reality is observed, evaluated, understood, and generalized. Consequently, identifying the research paradigm has significant implications as it will inform every single decision made in formulating the research study.

All research practitioners and theoreticians will agree that there are four concepts that need to be reviewed in order to clarify the research paradigm: 1) Ontology, 2) Epistemology, 3) Methodology, and 4) Methods. Scotland (2012) wrote a seminal piece that helps understand each one of these elements, and we will use his work to briefly review them.

1. Ontology: The study of a being, of a phenomenon (e.g., person, organization, weather-related event), and the assumptions we make in

order to determine whether this being is real or not (Scotland, 2012). For example,

a. Realism: The researcher feels compelled to have direct and quantifiable evidence of the existence of a phenomenon in order to confirm it is real. The researcher is convinced that the phenomenon exists independently of any human being knowing about it or not. A center idea is that reality needs to be and can be measured. This ontology belongs to the Positivist Quantitative Paradigm.

b. Relativism: The researcher feels compelled to collect the stories of those who have experienced the phenomenon in order to gather an understanding in a more indirect way. The researcher is convinced that reality is subjective and that it differs across people. A center idea is that reality needs to be constructed. This ontology belongs to the Interpretivist Qualitative Paradigm.

2. Epistemology: It is the study of knowledge and the processes by which knowledge is generated. This is knowledge about the being or phenomenon we mentioned earlier.

a. Objectivism: The researcher assumes that whatever meaning is associated to the phenomenon resides within the phenomenon and that this "can be captured by factual and descriptive language" (Scotland, 2012, p. 12). This epistemology belongs to the Positivist Quantitative Paradigm.

b. Subjectivism: The researcher assumes that whatever meaning is associated to the phenomenon it resides in the minds of those who experience it. Consequently, meaning is not discovered but constructed "from the standpoint of individuals who are participating in it" (Scotland, 2012, p. 14). This epistemology belongs to the Interpretivist Qualitative Paradigm.

3. Methodology: It is the technical approach used to demonstrate that a phenomenon *exists* and *means* something. What evidence should the researcher gather about the phenomenon?

a. Realism/Objectivism: The researcher is focused on identifying the phenomenon's component variables and the relationships that exist among them. The overall goal is to formulate laws that could help predict and generalize the occurrence of the phenomenon to the population at large (Scotland, 2012). The data collected can be used to confirm or challenge an existing theory about the phenomenon. Quantitative research methods are used. This methodology belongs to the Positivist Quantitative Paradigm.

b. Relativism/Subjectivism: The researcher is focused on investigating the cultural contexts where people live and have experienced the phenomenon of study. The phenomenon is described in great detail and the thick data collected can support the formulation of a new theory about the phenomenon. Qualitative methods are used. This methodology belongs to the Interpretivist Qualitative Paradigm.

4. Methods: This refers to the tools used to collect data that will support the process of knowing that a phenomenon exists and means something.

a. Realism/Objectivism: The researcher considers most appropriate to use experiments, conduct direct observations, randomization of participants, control variables, control/comparison groups, use standardized testing, closed-ended questionnaire questions, standardized observation tools, descriptive statistics, and inferential statistics to generalize sample results to the population. The specific research designs to choose from are: experimental, quasi-experimental, single-subject, correlational, survey research, and causal-comparative (a.k.a. *ex post facto*). These methods and research designs belong to the Positivist Quantitative Paradigm.

b. Relativism/Subjectivism: The researcher considers most appropriate to use open-ended interviews, focus groups, open-ended questionnaires, open-ended observations, think aloud protocols, role playing, and use content analysis of text or transcribed data from recordings. The specific research designs to choose from: case study, phenomenology, hermeneutics, and ethnography. These methods and research designs belong to the Interpretivist Qualitative Paradigm.

The researcher must determine which paradigm better suits the view of the world this person has, the phenomenon that exists, and how to generate understanding about it. From the preceding section it can be deduced that there are two main research paradigms: a) the Positivist Quantitative Paradigm and b) the Interpretivist Qualitative paradigm. There is a third, more eclectic in nature: c) the Pragmatist Mixed Methods Paradigm and lastly, a fourth d) the Critical Paradigm, which brings attention to the issue that knowledge is not value free and that individuals have cultural, racial, and political agendas embedded in the process of knowledge generation. Table 4.1 presents a summary of all of this information to support researchers in determining the research paradigm that best fits their research.

Table 4.1. Research Paradigm: Ontology, Epistemology, Methodology, and Methods.

Paradigm Components	Positivist Quantitative Paradigm	Pragmatist Mixed Methods Paradigm	Interpretivist Qualitative Paradigm
Ontology	Realism	Pragmatism	Relativism
Epistemology	Objectivism		Subjectivism
Methodology	QUANTITATIVE Focused on establishing cause-effect relationships, associations, laws, generalizations, and predictions. Goal to test theories. Deductive reasoning/ Theory verifying methodology (Creswell, 2004)	Combination QUANTI > QUALI QUALI > QUANTI QUANTI > Quali QUALI > Quanti Real-world Practice oriented methodology (Creswell, 2004)	QUALITATIVE Focused on investigating the cultural contexts which people inhabit. Goal to generate theories. Inductive reasoning/ Theory generating methodology (Creswell, 2004)
Methods	Quantitative tools: standardized testing, direct observations, questionnaires, structured interviews, achievement tests, self-checklists, attitude scales, personality tests, or rating scales.	Combination	Qualitative tools for recording personal narratives, open-ended interviews, focus groups, or think aloud protocols.
Data	Numeric data Descriptive and inferential statistics.	Combination	Text data Thematic interpretation of data.
Research Design	Experimental Causal-comparative Correlational Survey	Combination	Phenomenology Historical Narrative Case Study Grounded Theory

*Critical Paradigm
"Researchers have an agenda of change; therefore, it is often not supported by existing regimes" (Scotland, 2012, p. 14)

This paradigm assumes the following:
"Knowledge is both, socially construed and influenced by power relations from within society."
"What counts as knowledge is determined by the social positional power of the advocates of that knowledge."
"No research methodology is value-free."
"Reality is alterable by human actions."
"It aims to emancipate the disempowered."
(Scotland, 2012, pp. 14–16)

This table was developed based on Creswell (2004) and Scotland (2012).

Table 4.2. Qualitative and Quantitative Research Designs.

Qualitative Research Designs		
Ethnography	*Case Study*	*Phenomenology*
The study of cultural groups over an extensive amount of time	In-depth study of events over an extensive amount of time	The study of individual's experiences
Quantitative Research Designs		
Experimental	*Single-Subject*	*Correlational*
The study of the effect of an independent variable on a dependent variable on at least two groups.	The study of the effect of an independent variable on a dependent variable on a single individual or a single group.	The study of the association that naturally exists between the predictor variable and the outcome variable on a single group.
Causal-Comparative	*Survey*	*Action Research*
The study of the effect of a predictor variable on an outcome variable on at least two naturally occurring groups.	The descriptive study of one or more variables.	Can take the form of any of the described designs. The study is relevant to the practitioner's professional community.
Mixed Methods		
Sequential Exploratory	*Triangulation*	*Sequential Explanatory*
The study starts with a QUAL phase which generates the instrument to collect data during the second QUAN phase.	All data are collected at about the same time	The study starts with a QUAN phase for data collection and the data are brought to the QUAL phase for interpretation.

This table was developed based on Fraenkel et al. (2019).

Table 4.2 presents a brief description of the most common quantitative and qualitative research designs. This table is by no means comprehensive; the researcher should study more about each design in order to make a decision about which one would be the best fit for the study.

Textboxes 4.4 (Kristjansson-Nelson, 2020a, p. 151), 4.5 (O'Connell, 2020, p. 72), and 4.6 (Burkland, 2020, p. 59) present research design statements from recently published dissertations. They will provide you with an idea about how to describe the design of the study. Lastly, something that is extremely important to keep in mind relates to the fact that researchers need to keep in consideration that "different designs have

---

TEXTBOX 4.4.

Research Design Statement: Qualitative

A qualitative study was designed using grounded theory methodology that included data collection of interviews, focus groups, observations, and analysis of documents. After data collection, data analysis was performed on transcripts using open, axial, and selective coding.

TEXTBOX 4.5.

Research Design Statement:
Mixed Methods Sequential Explanatory

Design of the Study

This research project used a mixed-methods sequential explanatory design to analyze the effect of a summer literacy program on students' reading outcomes and their motivation to read. The study combined both quantitative and qualitative data to provide a voice to the participants for whom the study was created to support. STAR reading scores were analyzed to measure reading growth and questionnaire responses were analyzed to measure student and parent perceptions of learning, motivation, and elements of the Literacy Academy.

TEXTBOX 4.6.

Research Design Statement: Mixed Methods

Rationale for Convergent Mixed-Methods Research Design

Creswell and Plano Clark (2011) explained that a mixed-methods approach is one where "Researchers situate numbers in the contexts and words of participants, and they frame the words of participants with numbers, trends, and statistical results" (p. 21). A variety of mixed-methods approaches exist, but the researcher selected a convergent methodology given the types of data explored.

different reporting needs associated to them" (APA, 2020, p. 31). Guide-lines on how to present the results according to the type of research design utilized in a study will be presented in Chapter 5 in great detail.

SETTING

The setting refers to the location where the research will take place. If the study will recruit human subjects, then the setting refers to the communities where these individuals reside, the organizations where they work, centers where they go to study, in general any locale where they will execute the behavior of interest for the study. A detailed description of the geographical location (e.g., Midwest, border state), nature (e.g., boarding school, public school, community college, 4-year college), and demographics (e.g., 2,000 graduate students, 50% im-migrant, 100% in Free/Reduced Lunch Program, rural city with 5,000 habitants) should be provided. The researcher should carefully think in terms of any other descriptors of setting that may be relevant for the study due to its focus. For example, a study on women in the medical field that is conducted at a regional institution of higher education will have to include the breakdown of students, women and men, who have declared an interest in medicine-related programs (e.g., biology, chemistry, nursing). This information may not be relevant for a study on leadership traits among college students. The description of the set-ting should leave the reader with a clear idea about the physical, cul-tural, political, and social contexts where the study will be conducted (whenever pertinent). If participants will be recruited from different cities at a given state, then the researcher needs to describe the region. If participants will be recruited from states across the nation, then the researcher should describe the nation as the setting. Researchers must continue with the same logic if the study will recruit international par-ticipants. Textboxes 4.7 (Burkland, 2020, p. 58) and 4.8 (Leland, 2020, p. 57) provide actual descriptions of settings.

TEXTBOX 4.7.
Setting Description: Corporate Learning Environment

Research Site Profile

This mixed-methods study focused on understanding learning satisfaction in synchronous online classrooms within the corporate learning environment. For this study, a nationally recognized Fortune 125 (as of 2017) financial institution was selected as a research site. This institution had just over 45,000 employees across the globe and is headquartered in the United States. Given the broad geographic sprawl of the organization, technology is a growing area of emphasis in the delivery of training to reduce travel costs and increase access to diverse development opportunities.

TEXTBOX 4.8.
Setting Description: Public School

Context of the Study

This research took place within Fairbault Public Schools (FPS), which is a rural, midwestern school district located in southcentral Minnesota. Primarily as a result of multiple manufacturing and agricultural employment opportunities in this locality, the population of Fairbault has been steadily increasing in diversity. In particular, the Somali refugee population has been drawn to this area for employment reasons and family reunification.

PARTICIPANTS

In the social sciences, almost all research projects are focused on social phenomena, which have been classically defined as events that occur "whenever an individual capable of awareness and of interpreting the activities of similar individuals either immediately or mediately, directly or indirectly, irrespective of the limitations of time or space influences or is influenced by another" (Gillette, 1927, p. 571). Describing "participants' characteristics can be important for understanding the nature of the sample and the degree to which results can be generalized" to the population (APA, 2020, p. 83) and also for the purpose of replicating the study. In the minimum, the reader should learn the basic demographic information of participants: age, sexual orientation and gender identity (SOGI), socioeconomic status, ethnicity, and level of education. If participants are minors, additional demographic information would be considered crucial: family structure, developmental information, and disability status, for example. Importantly, depending on the research question(s), other relevant traits associated to the variables of study should be included. For example, immigrant status, minority status, number of children, among many other possible important demographic characteristics. The researcher needs to keep in mind that the phenomenon being studied will be impacted by *who* the participants are. Because of that, the more that is known about the participants, the more elements of analysis will be available to the researcher when the time comes to interpret the data. Textboxes 4.9 (Bradbury et al., 2012, p. 8) and 4.10 (Bradbury et al., 2012, p. 1138) show descriptions of participants in the White Earth Comprehensive Study. The former describes participants as centers providing services to young children. The latter describes participants as youth in the White Earth Reservation.

TEXTBOX 4.9.
Participants Description

Participants

Requests for information about early childhood education were sent to three tribal programs, to the seven schools still participating in the White Earth Comprehensive Education Study, and to one non-tribal Head Start Program with classrooms on the reservation. The three tribal early childhood programs responded to requests for information: White Earth Head Start Programs, White Earth Child Care Program, and White Earth Early Intervention. Two schools and one non-tribal Head Start program also responded to requests for information: Bagley School Readiness Program and Early Childhood Family Education, Waubun-Ogema School Readiness Kick Start Program, and MAHUBE Head Start Program. Four schools responded to specific requests about kindergarten assessment information: Detriot Lakes, Waubun-Ogema, Circle of Life, and Bagley.

TEXTBOX 4.10.
Participants Description: Youth

WE Youth

WE Youth were defined by Phase I of the CSEERSWE as White Earth Reservation children (birth through 18 years) who reside on or near the reservation. WE youth were also identified by Phase I of CSEERSWE using terms such as *adolescence, teen, school-age, pre-school, toddler,* and *infant* (Moshier, Wright, Bergland, & Dobmeier, 2009). WE professional stake-holders were defined by Phase I of CSEERSWE as (a) WE tribal council leaders, (b) WE K–12 school administrators, (c) WE K–12 educators, and (d) WE health care professionals.

A requirement when describing the participants in the study relates to the inclusion (i.e., Who is in and why?) and exclusion criteria (i.e., Who is out and why?) in the study. The inclusion criteria are defined as the key features of the target population that the researcher will use to answer their research questions. In contrast, the exclusion criteria are defined as features of the potential study participants who meet the inclusion criteria but present additional characteristics that could interfere with the success of the study or increase the risk for an unfavorable outcome (Patiño & Ferreira, 2018, p. 84). Textbox 4.11 (Bradbury et al., 2012, p. 1157) shows a sample of an inclusion as well as exclusion criteria. Lastly, before participants can be recruited, the researcher must receive training on how to conduct ethical research with human subjects (e.g., CITI). This training secures the protection of human participants in research, guaranteeing that none is placed at any psychological or physical risk resulting from joining the study. This is a training requirement that must be repeated every three years.

TEXTBOX 4.11.

Participants' Inclusion and Exclusion Criteria

The inclusion criteria for WE professional stakeholder participation included: (a) must be over the age of 18 years, (b) must be a WE tribal leader, educator, school administrator, health care provider (non-school), or health care provider (school). The health care providers from IHS, Mahnomen Health Center, and schools may have included: (a) physicians, (b) advanced practice nurses, (c) nurses, (d) nurse aides, and (e) paraprofessionals.

Study exclusions were: (a) those health care professionals no longer employed in their position, (b) health care professionals under the age of 18 years, and (c) those participants who chose not to take part in the survey. No participants under the age of 23 years were recorded in the survey responses.

Sampling Procedures

Sampling is the process of selecting the participants for the study (i.e., the sample), the group from which the data to address the research question(s) will be obtained (Fraenkel et al., 2019). In a positivist quantitative research paradigm, sampling is an important process because the focus of the study will be to generalize traits from the sample (i.e., statistics) to the population (i.e., parameters). Populations are large groups of individuals who share certain characteristics that are of interest to the researcher due to the nature of the study (e.g., women presidents of 4-year colleges, single-man mathematicians, children with an identified disability). Because oftentimes populations are too large to be studied entirely, the researcher needs to study a smaller group of individuals making this a more efficient approach. This smaller group is called a *sample*. Having said that, it is not unheard-of that in some few instances entire populations are studied (e.g., all high school students in Cass County), these are large-scale census research studies that their complexity make them the exception rather than the norm.

The researcher needs to provide a description of the sampling procedures planned to be used in the study. Textbox 4.12 (Bradbury et al., 2012, p. 46) provides a detailed description of one of the samples selected in the White Earth Comprehensive Study (Bradbury et al., 2012). In addition to

TEXTBOX 4.12.
Sample

1. Native American Students in Grades 3 through 5: A total of 278 students participated in this study (58% were boys). The sample was comprised of 32% of students in the third grade, 39% in the fourth grade, and 20% in the fifth grade. The majority of students received free lunch (65.1%) and approximately one fourth of them lived with both biological parents.

   While approximately half of this group had never been involved in disciplinary problems (46%), 13% had received a minimum of six and up to 36 disciplinary sanctions. Absenteeism or tardiness were not prevalent in this group, about 25% of students were absent from school between 10 and 41 times, and 18% of them arrived late at school between 10 and 89 times.

2. White Students in Grades 3 though 5: A total of 608 students participated in this study (53% were boys). The sample was comprised of 29% of students in the third grade, 29% in the fourth grade, and 25% in the fifth grade. About half of the group was in either a free (22%) or reduced (10%) lunch program and approximately two thirds of them (66%) lived with both biological parents.

   Disciplinary data were significantly unavailable for this group and we cannot determine whether it was an omission in the data collection process or whether there were no data to report, in which case each student could have received a "zero" score on this variable; however, that was not the case. Approximately 18% of students were absent from school between 10 and 26 times.

describing general demographic information (e.g., SOGI, socioeconomic status), it also describes other variables of interest for this study (e.g., absenteeism, tardiness). These descriptions, whenever possible, should be accompanied by descriptive statistics (e.g., frequencies, percentages).

In an interpretivist qualitative research paradigm, sampling is not a critical element since studies are not concerned with representativeness and generalization of results from the sample to the population.

One important question the researcher will eventually ask is this: How many participants are enough for the study? Sample size is an important issue and depends upon a number of important elements (Arriola, 2012). Consider the following questions:

1. Is a positivist quantitative research paradigm being utilized?
2. Is there a need to test a hypothesis (i.e., the study is confirmatory in nature)?
3. Will inferential statistics be used to test the hypothesis?
4. Will the sample be randomly selected?

If the answers to these questions are all "yes," then the researcher needs to calculate the sample size for the study. There are several formulas to do this and there are also electronic calculators for doing it. If a secondary data analysis will be conducted, then the SPSS software can be used to calculate the sample size instead of running calculations with the entire database. Table 4.3 shows the elements that need to be kept in mind when calculating the sample size if studying a phenomenon from the positivist quantitative research paradigm and when comparing two groups' means to measure the effect size of an intervention. Make sure to provide a description of your plans to determine the sample size of your study.

The formula that would need to be used to calculate the sample size, again for a study comparing two means (very common in education), is:

$$N = \frac{2(Z\alpha + Z\beta)^2 \, S^z}{d^2}$$

There are some missing values in this formula: a) The variance (S2) needs to be extracted from the literature and b) the level of impact

Table 4.3. Components to Calculate Sample Size When Comparing Two Means.

Component	Non-Directional Hypothesis	Directional Hypothesis
Confidence Level	95%	95%
Significance Level (α)	.05 / 1.96[*]	.05 / 1.645[*]
Power (1-β)	.80 / .842[*]	.80 / .842[*]
S^2	X[a]	X[a]
d^2	Y[b]	Y[b]

Source: Navarro (2020).

(*d*) needs to be determined by the researcher, in terms of what is the minimum difference between both means that the researcher would expect to obtain as a result of the study. Again, this formula is used when randomization is a methodological sampling option. For example, in educational research oftentimes non-random sampling is used due to the type of social phenomena that are frequently studied. For studies in which randomization is not possible, using this formula is always best practice to establish a point of reference from which to strategize the collection of an adequate sample size. For example, if the formula results in a sample size of 90 individuals, doubling or tripling that size to 180 or 270 would be a good compensatory approach. Having said that, some authors have offered a couple of good additional suggestions: a) to use a stratified convenience sampling (Knaub, 2017) or b) a homogeneous convenience sampling, "samples that are intentionally limited to specific sociodemographic subgroups and therefore homogeneous on one or more sociodemographic factors" (Jager et al., 2017, p. 20). When exploring the best course of action, the researcher needs to consider the logistics involved in each one of these alternatives.

The researcher must provide a detailed description of the procedures used to select the sample. There are two basic types of sampling procedures: a) random sampling and b) non-random sampling, and each one has different strategies (see table 4.4). Random sampling allows the researcher to use probabilistic statistics to test the study's hypothesis. In this type of sampling, every single member of the population has an equal chance of being selected (Navarro, 2020). In non-random sampling, on the other hand, there is no specific probability of being selected and the researcher may need to use non-parametric statistics to test the research hypothesis. The limitation with non-random sampling

Table 4.4. Sampling Types.

Random / Probabilistic	*Non-random*
• Simple random sampling (i.e., equal chance of being selected)	• Systematic sampling (i.e., every *n*th)
	• Convenience sampling (i.e., available)
• Stratified random sampling (i.e., strata, %)	• Purposive sampling (i.e., cherry pick based on researcher's judgment)
• Cluster random sampling (i.e., intact classes)	
• Systematic, two-stage random sampling (i.e., class first and randomization of a number per class second)	

Source: Fraenkel et al. (2019).

processes is that there is no way to estimate the representativeness of the sample to the population. Non-probabilistic samples may be skewed in some traits over others and consequently its level of generalization of findings to the population is significantly limited. Regardless of the type of sampling used, potential threats to the internal validity of the study should be addressed (e.g., attrition or loss of sample subjects). External validity threats (i.e., inability to generalize) arise when the researchers draw incorrect generalizations from the sample data to other people different from the sample, other settings, and past or future situations (Creswell, 2014). The researcher needs to be aware of these method-ological internal validity threats, which are specific to each design, and describe what procedures will be implemented to counter their impact as well as describe how the researcher will address any potential threats to the external validity of the study.

Best practices in research methods call for a description of the *target population*, which is the population where the phenomenon of interest occurs and from where the researcher will extract the sample. A detailed description of the target population serves the purpose of delineating the boundaries for inclusion and exclusion of potential par-ticipants in the study (i.e., sample). That is, decisions about who should participate and who should not will be determined by knowing well the characteristics of the target population. Textbox 4.13 shows the descrip-tion of the target population in the White Earth (Bradbury et al., 2012) comprehensive study.

TEXTBOX 4.13.
Population Description

Population Description

The population for this study was WE professional stakeholders over 18 years of age, and included the following: (a) WE tribal council leaders, (b) We K–12 school administrators, (c) WE K–12 educators, and (d) WE health care providers. This target population has strong social interac-tions with WE youth. The value of these relationships is vital to the WE youth and WE community. WE professional stakeholders hold an impor-tant position to preserve and nurture WE youth and serve as catalysts for implementing change. WE professional stakeholders may be able to identify areas of concern that can benefit We youth and the community.

Estimating the total target population of WE professional stakeholders was difficult (Joan LaVoy was contacted to retrieve population numbers of survey and emailing information). The WE reservation covers a vast area and is served by five counties including: (a) Mahnomen, (b) Becker, (c) Norman, (d) Polk, and (e) Clearwater. The accessible population for WE Phase II Health Arm will consist of school professionals (K–12 educators and K–12 administrators), WE tribal council leaders, and health care professionals (physicians, advanced practice nurses, nurses, and nurse aides in the school system and health care systems that serve in the WE community). This sample of potential participants was determined the most likely to witness the impact of the health concerns affecting the WE youth within the schools and in the community.

INSTRUMENTATION

Instrumentation relates to the tools used for data collection. "Scientific explanations demand ample observation and critical thinking" (Morales-Bermudez, 2011, p. 250). In the positivist quantitative research paradigm, the researcher must clearly identify the variables of study contained in each one of the research questions (i.e., dependent variable or outcome variable, independent variable or predictor variable). Those variables need to be measured, that is, relevant data must be collected on each one of them in order to adequately respond to the research question(s). Variables have the quality of variation, hence their name. For example, responding to a question about *marital status*, participants can answer: a) married, b) divorced, c) single, or d) other (i.e., nominal variable). Likewise, the variable *pediatric depression* may be represented by a score that varies from 0 to 120, and parents may identify any score from that scale as representing their children's mental status (i.e., continuous variable). Another example, the variable *SES* can be Low, Middle, or High (i.e., ordinal variable). In a given sample, each participant will have a different response for each variable (e.g., some are married, others single, one participant will select a pediatric depression score of 24 while another will select a score of 98). Participants' responses to the same

Table 4.5.   Types of Variables.

Type of Variable/Data	Example
Nominal CATEGORICAL	Gender: Man, Woman, Non-binary/Non-conforming, Transgender, Prefer not to respond Marital Status: Married, Single, Divorced
Ordinal CATEGORICAL	Level of Education: Elementary, Middle School, Secondary College Status: Undergraduate, Graduate Month of Birth: January, February, March . . . December
Interval NUMERICAL	Weekly Income: 0 to $500, 501 to $1000, 1001 to $1500, 1501 to $2000 Head Circumference: 0 to 10 inches, 11 to 20, 21 to 30, 31 to 40
Ratio NUMERICAL[1]	Academic Achievement: MCA Reading Score Weigh at Birth: The actual weight in pounds Compassionate Leadership Scale: Score obtained on this instrument

Source: Suárez Sousa (2021).

questions will *vary*. The researcher needs to know what scales of measurement are used to collect data with the instruments selected for data collection (i.e., nominal, ordinal, interval, ratio, or continuous). Table 4.5 presents additional examples of variables and their scale of measurement; this information is quite important as it will allow the researcher to determine which statistical analysis can be conducted with the data collected. More information on this issue will be provided in Chapter 5.

For data collection purposes, the researcher should search for an existing instrument or develop one that aligns well to the research questions and describe the tool in great detail (e.g., purpose, number of items, answering choices). If the researcher finds an adequate existing instrument that can be used in the study, the researcher should feel comfortable reaching out to the author(s) to inquire about it and request authorization. The chances are very high that the author(s) will grant authorization for the instrument to be used for research purposes.

If no instrument exists, then the researcher will have to embark in the process of developing one for the study, which is not an impossible task. If the researcher decides to go that route, detailed information about this process must be provided. Textbook 4.14 (Bradbury et al., 2012, p. 1158) shows the description of variables included in a descriptive quantitative study. Textbox 4.15 (Bradbury et al., 2012, p. 1161) provides a description of the instruments utilized in the White Earth Comprehensive Study.

TEXTBOX 4.14.
Variables Description

Research Variables

In this quantitative descriptive study, independent and dependent variables are not applicable because an intervention was not implemented nor a relationship hypothesized. In this descriptive study, variables were simply referred to as research variables rather than independent or dependent. The research variables were identified in the research purpose and questions that will be measured. The research variables in this study included: (a) WE reservation, (b) WE youth, (c) WE professional stakeholders, (d) perceptions, (e) influencing factors, (f) accidental injuries, (g) obesity, (h) diabetes, (i) teen pregnancy, and (j) mental health. Demographic variables collected during the survey included age, gender, race/ethnicity, and category of relationship with WE youth. These variables were collected to identify if findings are applicable in future studies. Table 3 displays the connection between the theory, research variables, and measurements.

TEXTBOX 4.15.
Measurement Tools

Measurement Methods/Tools

Measurement tools specifically addressing the health concerns of WE youth were sparse and revealed in Chapter II. Due to lack of fitness among currently published tools, an author-developed measurement tool was used for the study to capture WE professional stakeholders' perceptions regarding the health of WE reservation youth. This data collection tool measured the variables pertaining to the WE stakeholders with specific focus on: (a) demographic data, (b) accidental injuries, (c) obesity, (d) diabetes, (e) teen pregnancy, and (f) mental health. A limitation of this measurement tool was the use of questions that may have captured themes about health other than the five specific topics of literature review. At the request of John LaVoy, WE education director, and additional area pertaining to prevention was added to gather extraneous theme data. These categorized themes became the question domains.

There were no known tools in existence that specifically measure all the variables of interest in a single questionnaire. The author-developed tool incorporated culturally appropriate questions to extract the data relevant to the study and population.

Regardless of whether the instrument was developed by the researcher or by somebody else and unless the tool collects data on participants' opinions, there needs to be information regarding the *technical quality* of the instrument to ensure that the internal validity of the study will not be jeopardized. Only data collected from technically adequate instruments—that is, instruments that are valid and reliable—can lead to meaningful data interpretations and new understandings of the phenomenon being studied. This strengthens the study's internal validity.

Regarding reliability, Dimitrov et al. (2001) stated,

> [Reliability] provides important information regarding how repeatable the observations or scores are when (a) different people conduct the measurement, (b) using different instruments that purport to measure the same trait, and (c) there is incidental variation in measurement conditions. (p. 159)

According to Dimitrov, "reliability of any measurement is the extent to which the measurement results are free of random errors" (p. 260). Validity "has to do with whether an instrument measures what it purports to measure" (Dimitrov et al., 2001, p. 162). According to Cronbach (1979, as cited in Dimitrov, 2012), it is not the instrument that is validated but "the interpretation of data arising from a specified procedure" (p. 41). That is, validity refers to the ability of the instrument to support the researcher to "draw meaningful and useful inferences from the scores" (Creswell, 2014, p. 206).

If instruments that are valid and reliable become adapted or changed in any way in order to better align to the purpose of the study (e.g., it is too long for children; let's remove some questions), the instrument's validity and reliability will be negatively impacted and the quality of the study's data will be diminished. In other words, the data analysis and interpretation that results may be significantly questioned. The researcher, however, should feel empowered to adapt or change an existing valid and reliable instrument so that it will better align to the study's research question(s) bearing in mind that when this happens the researcher must conduct validity and reliability studies to ensure that the new version (or the newly created instrument) is indeed technically sound. Textbox 4.16 shows a description of the validity study plan for the Appraisal of Academic Influences Inventory (Bradbury, 2005) used in the White Earth Comprehensive Study (Bradbury et al., 2012). Textbox 4.17 shows a description of the reliability studies plan for the same instrument.

TEXTBOX 4.16.
Validity Study Plan

Content Validity Analysis Report of the
White Earth Student Surveys

Contents
Part I: Introduction and brief description of the process
Part II: Report for WE Survey—Grades 3 through 5
Part III: Report for WE Survey—Grades 6 through 12
Part IV: Suggestions

Part I: Introduction and brief description of the process

In measurement, content validity can be defined as the empirical evidence, provided by subject matter experts, that demonstrates the items (e.g., questions) of a given instrument are appropriate to its intended measurement concept and target population. As such, a high coefficient of content validity of a given instrument will be critical in ensuring that the data collected with such instrument will yield valid results. In this context, *valid results* refer to information that accurately represents the target population along the measurement concept (e.g., student self-perception).

For the present content validity analysis, five subject matter experts (SMEs) participated in the rating of the items/statements of two of the instruments utilized in the Education on the WE Indian Reservation Study (i.e., WE Student Survey—Grades 3 through 5 and WE Student Survey Grades 6 through 12). Subject matter experts are individuals who have vast knowledge in the measurement concept.

TEXTBOX 4.17.
Reliability Study Plan

Reliability Analysis Report

WE Survey—Grades 3 through 5

<u>Contents</u>
Part I: Introduction and brief description of the process
Part II: Coefficients of reliability and Cronbach's α (Alpha) per scale
Part III: General coefficient of reliability
Part IV: Conclusions

Part I: Introduction and brief description of the process

Reliability is a measure of the consistency of the results obtained with an instrument and repeated trials. This means that a student taking the WE Student Survey—Grades 3 through 5 today and then in two weeks' time—will obtain similar scores on both occasions. If an instrument has been demonstrated to be reliable, and changes in results are observed, these changes are said to be the result of an intervention. Because of this, demonstrating that an instrument has a high coefficient of reliability is strongly desired, particularly in the field of education where interventions for performance improvement are a part of periodic operations.

For the present reliability analysis, the internal consistency method (i.e., split-half reliability) was utilized. The steps in this process were as follows:

1. Data from 50 students who are randomly selected and entered into an Excel spreadsheet.
2. Text data (i.e., yes, no) were transformed into numeric data (i.e., 1, 0).
3. Composite variables were created for the following:

   a. Each one of the WE service skills (six in total)
   b. WE Survey as a whole

For best practices, the researcher is required to report the coefficients of validity and reliability obtained after conducting these reliability and validity studies. The researcher is also required to conduct the validity and reliability studies prior to conducting the main study. If an existing instrument is used without any modifications, the researcher must also report the validity and reliability coefficients provided by the authors. Lastly, the literature review should also include a section that describes the instruments used in the study when these instruments are commercially produced.

Within the interpretivist qualitative research paradigm, the main *instrument* for data collection is the researcher himself/herself. Because of that, validity and reliability have a different connotation. Both refer to the process the researcher follows when collecting data and giving meaning to the findings. This means that "the researcher checks for accuracy of the findings by employing certain procedures" (Creswell, 2014, p. 251). Validity in qualitative research denotes the level of trustworthiness and credibility of the findings (Creswell, 2014) while reliability means that "the researcher's approach is consistent across different participants and different projects" (Gibbs, 2007, as cited by Creswell, 2014, p. 251). Once again, regardless of paradigm, the researcher needs to provide a description of the strategies utilized to ascertain the quality of the data collection process.

DATA ANALYSIS

"The separation of relevant and non-relevant factors constitutes the principle of knowledge generation" (Morales-Bermudez, 2011, p. 250). The process of data analysis allows for careful mining of an abundance of information collected from participants. This is done in order to determine whether or not what the researcher observed was an event that occurred with regularity across a significant group of participants. If that is the case, then the researcher could propose said event to be a general law provided that the external validity of the study has not been jeopardized in any way. This important process generates new understanding about the phenomenon of study. If the study was designed within a positivist quantitative research paradigm, the researcher will need to describe the data analysis plan and procedures in alignment to the research question(s). A description of what descriptive statistics will be used and why they will be used over others needs to be provided along a description of the inferential statistics the researcher is planning to use. In both cases the researcher needs to justify the reasons why one test is used over any other one.

The Statistical Packet for the Social Sciences (SPSS) software is regularly utilized to analyze quantitative data. The researcher must describe how the data were populated into the SPSS database while describing the strategies that were used to ensure the confidentiality of participants. Chapter 5 provides detailed descriptions of a variety of data analyses that can be run with the SPSS software and that are commonly used in social science research along with useful tips for the creation of tables and figures that are instrumental in summarizing the data and communicating their meaning.

If the study was designed within an interpretivist qualitative research paradigm, the researcher will collect data that are mostly verbal (e.g., audio recorded responses to open-ended questions, video recorded focus groups, play actors' interjections) or in print (e.g., written responses to surveys, emails, books, manuals, movie scripts, field notes). These data represent explicit or inferred communications and the goal of researchers is to interpret these data through "the systematic classification process of coding and identifying themes or patterns" (Hsieh & Shannon, 2005, p. 1278). The most commonly used strategy for qualitative data analysis is *content analysis*, and there are different approaches to conduct it. More information about qualitative data analysis will be presented in Chapter 7. Once again, the researcher needs to provide a good deal of detail so that the reader will know what data analyses you have planned to conduct and why.

An important issue to consider during data analysis relates to researcher bias. "Every research needs to be designed, conducted, and reported in a transparent way, honestly and without any deviation from the truth. Research which is not compliant with those basic principles is misleading" (Šimundić, 2013, p. 12). Conducting research requires reporting the findings with integrity. Accepting or rejecting a quantitative study's null hypothesis should not make a difference in terms of the worth of a study, and neither should it become a burden for the researcher who is thinking in terms of landing a job, going for tenure, or for a promotion. Researchers ought to be reminded that their responsibility is to describe social phenomena as these occur and that the outcomes per se should have no bearing on the growth of their professional career.

THE RESEARCH QUESTION AND HYPOTHESIS

The research question is the conductor of the research orchestra. The research question guides all the methodological activities so that it can be answered (Creswell, 2014). Research questions create a system of relationships among the variables of the study and present this system in a statement format. These questions are not conceived in a vacuum; rather, they result from the researcher's professional experience and/ or the review of the literature. Quantitative research questions "inquire about the relationships among variables that the investigator seeks to know" (Creswell, 2014, p. 188). Because all the variables contained in the research question need to be measured, it is extremely important that each one of these is well defined. The researcher must remember that readers of research will include individuals who are unfamiliar with the focus area of the study and its associated terminology. Because of that, each variable must be clearly defined. Best practices indicate that researchers should provide two types of variable definitions: a) constitutive and b) operational. Constitutive definitions are academic definitions retrieved from the literature, not from a dictionary. For example, "Somatization is 'the tendency to experience and communicate somatic distress and symptoms unaccounted for by pathological findings, to attribute them to physical illness and to seek medical help for them (Lipowski, 1988, p. 1359)" (Shannon et al., 2010). Operational definitions, on the other hand, indicate how the variable will be measured (for example, by using the Children's Somatization Inventory [CSI-24] developed by Walker et al. [2009]). The research question(s) needs to be clearly stated and should be accompanied by both definitions. Hypotheses are "predictions the researcher makes about the expected outcomes or relationships among variables" (Creswell, 2014, p. 188). These predictions will allow the researcher to infer the results from the sample to the population. The hypothesis of the study needs to be clearly stated. Textbox 4.18 (Bradbury et al., 2012, p. 1190) provides a sample of research questions. See Chapter 2 for additional guidelines on how to write research questions.

TEXTBOX 4.18.
Research Questions

Research Questions

The purpose of this quantitative study was to describe WE professional stakeholders' perception regarding health concerns that may impact academic performance success among WE American Indian youth (age 0–19 years) residing on or near the WE reservation.

The two research questions address the following: 1) What are WE professional stakeholders' perceptions regarding accidental injuries, obesity, diabetes, teen pregnancy, and mental health as notable concerns among WE youth? and 2) What are WE professional stakeholders' perceptions of factors influencing WE youth behaviors related to these health concerns?

PROCEDURES

In essence, this section should provide a detailed description of the steps taken in order to execute the study, that is, all the research-related activities carried on with the purpose of successfully completing it. The goal is to provide detailed information to facilitate the replication of the study by any other researcher. In that respect, the researcher must think of the relevant pieces of information that would support replication (e.g., identifying potential participants, following up on participants, planning and executing focus group sessions). This section should not overwhelm the reader with unnecessary details but facilitate an efficient replication of the study.

Table of Research Questions Alignment

When conducting a quantitative study, it is advisable to include a table of research questions and overall methodology alignment presenting every research question along several descriptors: 1) the variables (e.g., dependent variable, outcome variable), 2) design or strategy used to collect the data (e.g., in-depth interview, focus group, electronic questionnaire), 3) the instrument used to collect data for that

Table 4.6. Research Question(s) Alignment.

Research Question	Variables	Design	Instrument	Items	Validity & Reliability	Technique	Source
RQ1: What factors impact nutrition and dietetics professional in providing supervised practice experiences as preceptors in ASCEND accredited programs?	DV1: Willingness	Survey	Online Questionnaire (Appendix H)	Q3.2.1– Q3.2.11, Q6.9 Q 6.12	N/A	Online Survey	Nutrition and Dietetics Professionals
		Focus Group	Online Synchronous Focus Group (Appendix I)	1	N/A	Online Interview— Focus Group	Nutrition and Dietetics Professionals
	DV2: Satisfaction	Survey	Online Questionnaire (Appendix H)	Q4.2.11– 4.2.11	N/A	Online Survey	Nutrition and Dietetics Professionals
		Focus Group	Online Synchronous Focus Group (Appendix I)	2	N/A	Online Interview— Focus Group	Nutrition and Dietetics Professionals

Source: Brekken (2021, p. 45).

specific research question (if a single instrument is used to address several research questions, then identify the corresponding items), 3) validity and reliability of the instrument (i.e., when measuring a construct or attribute, if you are gathering participants' opinions then this would not be applicable), and 4) the source of the data (i.e., participants). This table ensures that the researcher accounts for all the important elements needed in order to address each one of the research questions successfully, and it provides confirmation that these elements are well aligned. Table 4.6 provides a sample of this table.

CONCLUSION

Once all the components of the Methods or Methodology chapter have been described in great detail in the preceding sections, the researcher needs to wrap up the chapter by providing a summary of what was described. This should focus fundamentally on reminding the reader what the phenomenon being studied is, as well as the significance of the inquiry. Briefly review the most salient characteristics of the methodology used for the inquiry (e.g., instrumentation, data analysis, sampling, setting). The researcher needs to think about this last paragraph as if this was the abstract of the preceding entire chapter or section. The last sentence or paragraph should provide a preview of what the following chapter will contain.

5

WRITING THE RESULTS

The results section of a dissertation, manuscript, or technical report is an essential component as it provides a clear view of the phenomenon the researcher is studying. By virtue of the data carefully collected in alignment to the research questions (RQ), the researcher will have the ability to depict the reality of this phenomenon in great detail. The goal is that the data provide a new understanding of the phenomenon of interest or corroborate an already described reality, if the study was a replication of previous research. "The results section should tell the reader how the data were analyzed and the results of this analysis" (Johnson & Christensen, 2017, p. 616). In order to accomplish this goal, data organization is of essence. The central idea is to "report the most relevant results [and] ensure that the results directly contribute to answering your original research questions or hypotheses" (APA, 2020, p. 372). Because data collection was formulated in direct alignment to the needs of the study's research questions and/or hypotheses (see table of research questions and overall methodology alignment in Chapter 4), the researcher should be equipped with all the necessary data to address each of these inquiries.

An important aspect of presenting the results is the fact that the researcher should not provide any interpretation or discussion just yet (that will come later). The responsibility when presenting the results is to share the data in a sequential, succinct, and clear manner. This presentation can be accompanied by theoretical support (i.e., references) whenever strategies of data analysis were used beyond what the researcher had originally proposed in the methodology chapter or section.

This chapter will help identify the most important elements required when presenting the results of the study and will review the following components: introduction, reporting results, and presenting data. Chapter 7 and Chapter 8 of this book will provide detailed information regarding qualitative and quantitative data analyses. This chapter focuses exclusively on the presentation of results.

INTRODUCTION

For dissertation purposes, the researcher should start this section by reminding the reader what was the purpose of the study. It is helpful to remember that some readers may only wish to read the results or any other chapter in isolation. Because of that, it is good practice to ensure that the introductory text of each chapter or section (besides the introductory component of the entire dissertation, report, or manuscript) provides a clear understanding of the problem and purpose of the study so that each can stand alone. This introductory piece must include the study's research questions and/or hypotheses, which are later used as headings to organize the presentation of the data. This introductory piece needs also to provide a detailed description of who the participants were. This could be accomplished through the inclusion of a table reporting participant demographic information. The goal is to ensure that the research questions and/or hypothesis are understood in the context of who the participants were.

REPORTING THE RESULTS

Systematic

There is a relatively fixed sequence that needs to be followed when presenting the results of a study, but different research designs require some unique considerations (Creswell & Clark, 2011). If this is a qualitative or an exploratory quantitative study, the presentation sequence is determined by the hierarchy of the research questions and the researcher should follow that order. That is, the primary research question(s) should be addressed first and then the researcher proceeds with addressing the secondary research questions. If this is a quantitative confirmatory study, start by addressing the study's null hypothesis and proceed following the hierarchy of research questions as described before. If this is a mixed methods study, it will depend on the specific design used. For example, if it is a sequential explanatory study the researcher will have to start with the quantitative data, which is the primary data set in this research design, followed by the qualitative data. The opposite occurs in a sequential exploratory study. If the study uses a triangulation design, there is no specific order to present the data; simply follow the hierarchy of the research questions. If the triangulation study has a single research question, then the researcher has the freedom to start with either data set. The theoretical or conceptual framework (see Chapter 2) can provide the direction as to the possible order to follow within this research design.

Within each research question, the researcher should start by providing a narrative response and then proceed to present the data, reporting the most relevant first. The length of the narrative is directly proportional to the amount of data that were collected. Some authors will make use of visual supports, such as tables and figures, adding to the overall length of the narrative. In qualitative studies, tables are used to showcase selected quotes from participants, and figures may present new conceptualizations of the phenomenon being studied. In quantitative studies, the results narrative is accompanied by tables or figures that help the researcher highlight the most salient findings.

Comprehensive

In general, "explain your findings and relate them to your problem, question and hypothesis" (Faryadi, 2019, p. 778), while providing the reader with all available elements to appraise the significance of the study. That is, the researcher should report *all* the data associated to each one of the research questions and/or hypothesis in *great detail*, creating a broad scope of understanding of the phenomenon being studied. There should be very compelling reasons why the researcher would leave parts of the data out of the reporting process (i.e., invalid). If that were the case, the researcher would need to provide a rationale accompanied by references that ensure theoretical support to this decision.

The researcher needs to keep in mind that even though the results should be written without making interpretations or discussing any part of it, this writing process will help the researcher identify the elements to be later discussed in connection to the current literature (i.e., agreement or disagreement with your results), the gaps in the literature, which will springboard the recommendations for further research as well as recommendations for practice. Because of that, the researcher must remain alert to the process of making those connections as results are organized.

While some narratives of results are lengthier than others just because of the amount of data collected, the worth of the study will not be measured by the number of pages written. Also, the results of the study may not coincide with what the researcher expected to find or what the literature had prognosticated. The role of the researcher is to report the findings, honoring the scientific methods used. Regardless of the results of the study, the researcher is contributing to the advancement of knowledge in that scientific area.

PRESENTING DATA

Outcomes/Findings

Qualitative Data

There are several elements that you need to keep in mind when reporting qualitative results. The researcher should start by reporting the software used to conduct the analyses (e.g., QDA Miner, Nvivo, SPSS Text Analytics) and the year of the version used. If the researcher conducted any data analysis differently from what was proposed in the methodology chapter or section, the researcher must provide a detailed description of what was done accompanied by one or more citations to support this decision. Then, the results need to be organized by research questions in a way that is "compatible with the study design"

(APA, 2020, p. 99), as indicated earlier in this chapter. Qualitative researchers may opt to analyze data without the assistance of an existing software, thus engaging in a more creative and less mechanical coding process (Denzin & Lincoln, 2003).

Creswell (1998) described how qualitative researchers use many different approaches when writing the narrative of results (e.g., by chronological order, by themes, by participants). Regardless of which approach is used, it is quite important to keep in mind a few important recommendations. First, the researcher must bring the voice of participants in the study by incorporating a variety of quotes, making sure to identify parenthetically which participant said what (e.g., Participant 6). Creswell (1998) has identified three different types of quotes: a) short and eye-catchy quotes provide evidence of particular perspectives, b) embedded quotes are phrases that support evidence for the existence of specific themes or common perspectives, and c) longer quotes are more complex and require the researcher providing guidance to the reader to identify the interplay of the many ideas presented. The researcher must be aware that quotes should not be used to "replace the description of the findings of the analysis" (APA, 2020, p. 99); that is the researcher's job to do in their own words. Second, the researcher must bring the voice of the researcher's *self* into the narrative (e.g., interpretative commentaries, own experiences or reflections) with the goal of weaving a narrative that contains the phenomenology of participants (i.e., *emic* perspective) as well as that of the researcher (i.e., *etic* perspective). Third, create what Johnson and Christensen (2017) describe as "vivid descriptions of the context, setting, participants, cultural scenes, and interactions among the participants" (p. 631) so that the reader can "vicariously experience what it is like to be in the same situation as the research participants" (p. 631). The American Psychological Association (2020) recommends researchers "present synthesizing illustrations (e.g., diagrams, tables, models), if useful in organizing and conveying findings" (p. 99).

Throughout the process of writing the narrative of results, it is quite important to incorporate standards of research quality and data verification. These can be accomplished by a) making sure the research questions were driving the data analysis, b) checking that the "analyses techniques are competently applied in a technical sense" (Creswell,

1998, p. 195), c) making explicit the researcher's assumptions as related to the phenomenon being studied (i.e., subjectivity, researcher bias), d) using thick descriptions to create transferability and corroboration of your findings, and e) using *member checks* at one or multiple points to allow the participants of your study to confirm the credibility of the data. The researcher "will need to find an appropriate balance between description and interpretation to write a convincing Results section" (Johnson & Christensen, 2017, p. 631). Most importantly, the level of detail provided will allow the researcher to confidently support the study's conclusions.

Lastly, it is important to remember that any supportive information that may not find a place in the narrative of results could still be included as an Appendix (e.g., comprehensive table of quotes).

Quantitative Data

There are several elements that the researcher needs to keep in mind when reporting the quantitative results. The researcher must start by reporting the software used to conduct the analyses (e.g., SPSS, Excel, Stata, R) and the year associated to the version used. The researcher should also describe the process of data entering (Streiner, 2007). For example, if a Qualtrics questionnaire was used to collect data, then a description must be provided of how the data were collected via email (i.e., with link to the questionnaire), downloaded from Qualtrics, uploaded onto SPSS, cleaned (e.g., outliers, recoding), and then analyzed. The same must be done for data collected in any other way (e.g., through direct observation of participants at work) or for secondary data used in the study (i.e., existing data collected by others). If there were any missing data, the researcher must report the frequency, the possible explanations for this occurrence (Johnson & Christensen, 2017), as well as the methods used to address this issue (make sure to provide citations to support your decisions). The American Psychological Association (2020) recommends providing "evidence and/or theoretical arguments for the causes of data that are missing" (p. 80). Then, as indicated before, the researcher should proceed to present the results organized by the hierarchy of the research questions.

While the specific narrative that answers a quantitative research question may not be extensive (i.e., one or two sentences), the contrary occurs with the description of the data analysis that accompanies this answer. For example, a quantitative research question may inquire about the potential relationship among a number of variables. While the narrative statement summarizing the findings may indicate that there was no significant relationship among those variables, the data presented should provide unequivocal evidence of that assertion and a narrative should help the reader understand said evidence. For that reason, the researcher needs to report all pertinent statistical tests conducted with the purpose of addressing this quantitative research question, making sure that no analyses are left out of the reporting process inadvertently.

In quantitative research, any statistically significant finding from any inferential test (e.g., t tests) should be accompanied by its respective notation, which includes "the numerical value of the test statistic along with the accompanying degrees of freedom, the exact probability level, and an indicator of the size and direction of the effect" (Johnson & Christensen, 2017, p. 616) as well as confidence intervals (Johnson & Christensen, 2017; Streiner, 2007). Note that any non-significant inferential test result does not require this detailed notation. Any descriptive statistics should include measures of central tendency (e.g., mean, median) as well as measures of variability (e.g., standard deviation, range).

It is also important to keep in mind that while the researcher may have planned to use inferential parametric tests to test the null hypothesis, it is only after the data have been collected when the researcher will be able to confirm whether parametric tests are valid to use or not. Because of this, the researcher must always confirm that the statistical assumptions associated to the parametric tests planned to be utilized in the study were met. If they were not, the researcher must opt to utilize the corresponding non-parametric alternative and accompany this decision with a written explanation addressing the violation of statistical assumptions.

Lastly, the researcher must remember that any important supportive information that may not find a place in the narrative of results could still be included as an Appendix (e.g., table with demographic information from each participant).

Tables and Figures

Tables and figures are important elements in academic writing and publishing as they economically communicate results that would otherwise require extensive narratives (Johnson & Christensen, 2017). Quite importantly, tables and figures should support the understanding of the study's results. In the fields of education and psychology, the American Psychological Association publishes periodically the *Publication Manual of the American Psychological Association*. This manual provides detailed descriptions of the requirements for the design of tables and figures. If the researcher is publishing research in the fields of education of psychology, the APA Manual should be reviewed when preparing a dissertation, paper, report, or presentation. Currently, the manual is in its 7th edition (APA, 2020), and this version includes two critical checklists. One addresses the most important requirements when developing tables (p. 207) and contains a list of 15 items (e.g., Are table notes, if needed, in the order of general note, specific note, and probability note? Are all tables called out or referenced to in the text?). The other checklist addresses the most important requirements when developing figures (p. 232), which contains 17 items (e.g., Are all figures numbered consecutively with Arabic numerals in the order in which they are first mentioned in the text? Are the magnitude, scale, and direction of grid elements clearly labeled?). Researchers must review both checklists.

In general, tables "should be used only when they can summarize or convey information better, more simply, or more clearly than text alone" (Fraenkel et al., 2019, p. 559), while figures "should be used only when they augment the text and can present the essential facts in a way that is clear and easy to understand" (Johnson & Christensen, 2017, p. 619). Both must always be referenced in the text by their title (e.g., table 14, see figure 3) and this title should briefly describe "what data it contains" (Johnson & Christensen, 2017, p. 618). Textboxes 5.1 (Bremer, 2020, p. 59) and 5.2 (Lundberg, 2020, p. 58) show the two different ways tables or figures can be referenced in the body of the narrative.

TEXTBOX 5.1.

Referencing a Table in Parenthesis

Finally, participants were asked where and when they were originally taught about rubrics and whether they have participated in learning about rubrics in professional development in-service activities or Professional Learning Communities (PLCs) within their district or otherwise. These questions helped me hear the stories of participants using and defining rubrics in context. The interview guide (Table 2) includes the questions asked to each participant.

When considering the use of figures to report the results of the study, the researcher should think of "drawings, graphs, charts, even photographs or pictures" (Fraenkel et al., 2019, p. 559). This range of options can bring quite a bit of flexibility for the researcher to present the data or other events associated with the study that are worth sharing with the reader. For example, figure 5.1 shows the photo of a handwritten note sent by an elementary student (i.e., research participant) to the researcher in the context of a research focusing on literacy skills. This figure is important as it provides the reader with a window into the participant's phenomenology during the conduction of the study.

TEXTBOX 5.2.

Referencing a Table in Text

Table 2 presents the rates of suspension per race/ethnic group at each length of suspension. For example, White students account for 43% of one day suspensions, whereas Black students account for 26% of one day suspensions, and, for reference, student demographics are included at the bottom of the figure. Black students, specifically, represent a greater percentage of suspensions as the number of days increase.

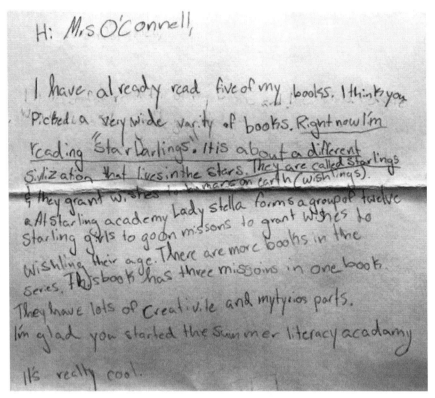

H: Mrs O'Connell,

I have already read five of my books. I think you picked a very wide varity of books. Right now I'm reading "Star Darlings". It is about a different sivlization that lives in the stars. They are called Starlings & they grant wishes. here on earth (wishings). A At Starling academy Lady Stella forms a group of twelve Starling girls to go on missons to grant wishes to Wishlings their age. There are more books in the series. This book has three missons in one book. They have lots of creativite and mytyios parts. I'm glad you started the Summer literacy acadamy. It's really cool.

Figure 5.1. Figure example.
Source: O'Connell (2020a, p. 182).

Figure 5.2 provides a snapshot of the participants engaged in research-related activities as the study was occurring. When human subjects are minors or are members of any other vulnerable population, researchers must protect their identity and avoid taking photos of their faces. If human subjects are adults, written consent would be required at the time of recruitment in order to publish photos that would allow their identification. The impact that figures like these generate on the reader is something that the researcher needs to consider when writing the narrative of results. The decision about what figures to include will depend on the phenomenon being studied and the narrative that the researcher wants to create.

Figure 5.2. Figure with photo.
Source: O'Connell (2020a, p. 227).

Qualitative Data

Qualitative research generates an abundance of text data collected through in-person or virtual interactions with participants (e.g., interviews, focus groups) or through other non-interactive means of data collection (e.g., observations). It is important that the researcher provides the reader with a list of participants along relevant demographic

Table 5.1. Participant Demographic Data.

Participant by Position	Gender	Years of Experience in Education	Teacher Leadership Position	Years
Principal	woman	17 (5 Principal)		
Q Comp Coordinator	woman	29	Coordinator	10
Elementary				
Kindergarten	woman	12		
1st Grade	woman	8	PLC Facilitator	2
2nd Grade	woman	2		
3rd Grade	woman	30	Peer Coach	7
High School				
Math	man	6		
Media/Science	man	17	Peer Coach (former)	6
Social Studies	man	6		
Language Arts	woman	7	Mentor	2

Source: Bockelmann (2021, p. 99).

information (e.g., gender, migration status). Table 5.1 provides a sample of a study regarding teacher leadership in which participants' demographic data that were reported were very pertinent to this study.

Since participants' quotes are essential in qualitative research, tables are used to present salient quotes along the themes that emerged from the data analysis. It is important that these tables provide clear identification of the authorship of each one of the selected quotes, as seen in table 5.2 (e.g., Mentor). Table 5.3 shows embedded quotes along the themes and the codes used in the development of the themes. Authorship is also clearly provided (e.g., Participant F).

In qualitative research, figures can also be used to describe the processes of data analysis or describe an innovative conceptualization of the phenomenon being studied, in part or whole. Figure 5.3 shows the process of data analysis in a grounded theory study, which resulted in the formulation of a new theoretical construct. Finally, in qualitative research, figures can be needed to "illustrate some complex theoretical formulation or represent the empirical result of a complex interaction" (Johnson & Christensen, 2017, p. 619). Figure 5.4 presents the complexity of text data analysis and the resulting systematization of codes used to categorize the data by the researcher.

Table 5.2. Qualitative Data Example 1: High School Participants' Responses to Purpose of the Teacher Leadership System.

Participant	Phrase	Theme
Social Studies Teacher	• To help you grow as a professional	Teacher Development
Social Studies Teacher	• We want teachers to be leading professional development of teachers	Teacher Development
Social Studies Teacher	• More honesty and growth oriented	Teacher Development
Mentor	• Take care of teachers' needs	Teacher Development
Math Teacher	• Empowering people	Teacher Development
Peer Coach (former)	• Continual process of improvement	Teacher Development
Principal	• Become better teachers	Teacher Development
Mentor	• To come together and have that support to work together	Collaboration
Peer Coach (former)	• More of a collaborative	Collaboration
Peer Coach (former)	• If we're all aligned . . .	Collaboration
Principal	• Teachers working in teams	Collaboration
Principal	• Want to be more collaborative	Collaboration
Principal	• Get teachers out of their silos	Collaboration/Unity
Mentor	• Working as a team instead of doing our own thing	Unity
Mentor	• Common ground	Unity
Math Teacher	• Empowering teams	Unity
Mentor	• To meet the students' needs	Student Needs
Peer Coach (former)	• It'll be a better experience for the kids	Student Needs
Principal	• Address student learning	Student Needs
Principal	• Help our kids get what they need	Student Needs

Source: Bockelmann (2021, p. 118).

Table 5.3. Qualitative Data Example 2: Qualitative Support for Virtual Focus Group Participants.

Theme	Code	Support Derived from Focus Group Participants
Training	Faculty Knowledge and Experience	*"I don't know that they see the violation in the classroom as clear cut as the scenarios in the questionnaire. They are not able to get there as quickly or as clearly as these scenarios are laid out. Perhaps if they could, we might see more actual reporting." (Participant F)*
		"What is the perceived level of understanding that each faculty member has regarding APA and plagiarism? Did they have specific training at another institution? It would be interesting to see how those faculty experience/expectations played into their decisions to report." (Participant A)
		"It would be interesting to learn what faculty consider to be an egregious offense, as this term often determines whether faculty submit an offense or not." (Participant H)
	Collaboration Challenges	*"Teachers are not sure if plagiarism happens in these spaces [group assignments]. This also leads to questions as to if students understand the boundary between working together and doing their own work, further complicating the situation for faculty." (Participant C)*
	Intentional vs. Non-Intentional Plagiarism	*"Faculty were more lenient in cases of inability to cite correctly versus a conscious decision to plagiarize." (Participant G)*

Source: Larson (2020, p. 93).

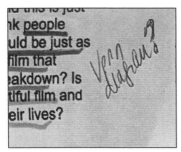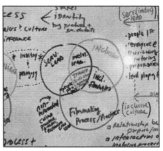

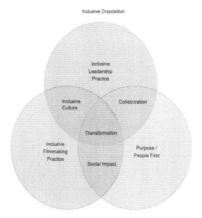

Note. Early in the process of labeling, a memo was made to explore relationships found in the data through a Venn diagram, which evolved over time.

Figure 5.3.   Process of data analysis.

Source: Kristjansson-Nelson (2020b, p. 21).

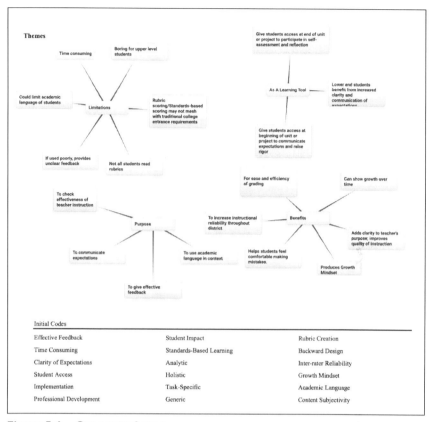

Figure 5.4.   Conceptual map.
Source: Bremer (2020, p. 5).

Quantitative Data

Quantitative research generates an abundance of numerical or coded data collected through in-person or virtual interactions with participants (e.g., interviews, questionnaires) or through other non-interactive means of data collection (e.g., observations, existing assessment data). Tables and figures are staples of quantitative research, and Johnson and Christensen (2017) indicate that "tables are preferred for presenting detailed quantitative data and illustrating main effects on multiple variables" (p. 617) while "figures can illustrate interactions effectively" (p. 617). See table 5.4, which presents descriptive statistics for a study on middle school students.

Table 5.4.   Descriptive Statistics: School-Level Comparison of Means by Survey Administration Year for Component Scales.

Component Scale	2016 Administration (pre)			2019 Administration (post)		
	N	M	SD	N	M	SD
Educational Engagement	552	8.60	1.957	566	8.42	1.806
Adult Connectedness	548	3.59	1.39	560	3.66	1.365
Community Connectedness	525	1.78	1.301	542	1.96	1.234
School Connectedness	518	5.71	2.292	534	5.68	2.298
Future Outlook	511	5.68	2.245	531	5.59	2.097
Self-View	514	3.52	1.762	534	3.54	1.641

Note: Educational engagement maximum score was 12 points; adult connectedness maximum score was 6 points; community connectedness maximum score was 4 points; School connectedness maximum score was 10 points; future outlook maximum score was 9 points; self-view maximum score was 6 points.

Source: Honetschlager (2020b, p. 17).

As indicated earlier in this chapter, tables with descriptive statistics should include measures of central tendency as well as measures of variability. As seen in textbox 5.3 (Honetschlager, 2020b, p. 23), descriptive and inferential test results can also be presented in narrative format. These narratives include prescribed content, some of which will change depending on the inferential test being used (e.g., ANOVA), while descriptive components remain the same across the board (i.e., mean values).

TEXTBOX 5.3.

Narrative of Results

Educational Engagement. Comparison of educational engagement component scale scores between the 2016 and 2019 survey administration show that at all levels, the mean educational engagement score decreased. Specifically striking is the decrease in mean educational engagement scores for the county level. Figure 2 presents a graphical comparison of mean educational engagement scores at all levels. The 2016 school education engagement score was $M = .19$, 95% CI [−.03 to .41] higher than the 2019 score; a Welch t-test revealed that this decrease was not statistically significant ($p = .099$). At the county level, the 2016 educational engagement score was $M = .44$, 95% CI [.31 to .57] higher than the 2019 score; this was a statistically significant difference in means ($p < .001$, $d = .24$). At the state level, the 2016 educational engagement score was $M = .37$, 95% CI [.35 to .39] higher than the 2019 score; this was also a statistically significant difference in means ($p < .001$, $d = .21$).

This narrative includes mean values, confidence intervals (i.e., CI), which generally speaking should reflect the 95% level of confidence (i.e., 2 SEMs) as well as the effect size for the inferential test being used. In the example provided in box 5.3, the inferential test was the Welsh test used to compare means (i.e., non-parametric) and Cohen's d used to determine effect size. Per the American Psychological Association (2020), all statistical symbols should be presented in italics (e.g., n, p). If the researcher is writing a dissertation and is uncertain as to how to determine some of these values, check with the research adviser.

While tables seem rather simple to design, they are one of the most common reasons why manuscripts are rejected (Frels et al., 2010). If the researcher is writing a dissertation or writing a manuscript in the fields of education or psychology, then the APA Manual should be used. If the researcher is writing a manuscript to be submitted for publication, then it is crucial to check if the journal adheres to the APA Manual or requires something different (e.g., MLA). The researcher should never make assumptions about publication requirements and should always take the time to read the guidelines provided to authors. The simplest way to create a table is by using the automatic table feature of Microsoft Word; all horizontal and vertical lines can be made invisible so that the researcher can later highlight with the *borders* feature only the lines required by APA (2020).

An important issue to keep in mind is that figures in general are prone to clutter, which is something the researcher needs to prevent. According to Knaflic (2015), clutter in figures "are visual elements that take up space but don't increase understanding [which] can contribute to excessive or extraneous cognitive load" (p. 73). In the world of data visualization, cognitive load is defined as "the mental effort that's required to learn new information [and clutter] takes up mental resources but doesn't help the audience to understand the information" (p. 72). In essence, the researcher must avoid making the graphs too complicated. The idea is not to demonstrate how capable the researcher is with graphic design but to communicate in an effective way the study's findings. Figure 5.5 clearly compares the score distributions of two groups of instructors (i.e., in-person, online synchronous). It is a figure that can easily be comprehended.

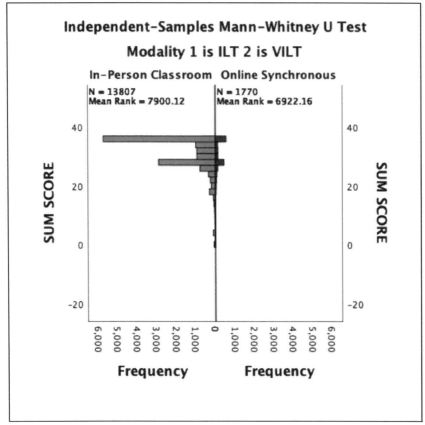

Figure 5.5.   Figure example of score distributions.
Source: Burklund (2020, p. 77).

Lastly, figures can also be utilized to represent a new conceptualization of the phenomenon or to represent the dynamics of the variables
being studied. Figure 5.6 shows the interplay of the variables being
studied to explain effective online instructional design practices. While
this interplay could be explained within a narrative, the figure creates
a more efficient option by systematizing a substantial number of elements and aiding the reader in understanding the findings. Additionally, the narrative that accompanies the figure should not describe it in
its entirety, but it should provide sufficient direction to help the reader
gain full understanding on their own. Figures allow "researchers from
different backgrounds to see and discuss phenomena in a way that might
not otherwise be possible" (Latour, 1990, as cited in Caissie et al., 2017,

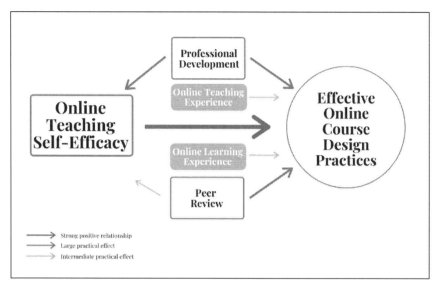

Figure 5.6.   New conceptualization diagram.
Source: McMahon (2021, p. 176).

p. 538). Indeed, figures have the power of encapsulating a substantial amount of information and as such are essential in the dissemination of the most fundamental findings of a given study.

It is important to remember that "an effective data visualization can mean the difference between success and failure when it comes to communicating the findings of your study" (Knaflic, 2015, p. 8). The researcher needs to invest time to think carefully how best to display the results by using tables or figures. As time is devoted to reviewing the literature relevant to the study, the researcher should pay close attention to the tables and figures utilized in those studies. Because those studies share similar inquiries, keeping a collection of screenshots or photos of tables and figures that are most relevant will be helpful to the researcher when the time comes to visually represent the study's results.

CONCLUSION

Writing the results of the study is a challenging process because the researcher will likely have a great deal of data to systematize. The researcher is reminded to follow the sequence determined by the hierarchy of the research questions and/or hypotheses and to support the reader's comprehension by using tables and figures. Also, the researcher must provide a great deal of detail when presenting the results so that any other researcher, if so inclined, could verify the researcher's claims (Faryadi, 2019). Caissie et al. (2017) remind us that the gap between the knowledge generated by the scientific activity and the practical application of this scientific knowledge can only be bridged by the ability to transfer knowledge from one to the other. That knowledge transference depends largely on the researcher's ability to clearly communicate the results of the study so that these results can gain practical significance (i.e., applicability).

6

WRITING THE DISCUSSION

The final chapter of one's dissertation is commonly referred to as the "discussion chapter." Although the last chapter of a dissertation will likely be one of the shorter ones, it may prove the most impactful in many ways since it involves a summary of the findings, an explanation of what those findings mean, and recommendations for practice. As Sampson (2017) noted, "The discussion has the potential to be the most satisfying, interesting, and meaningful aspect of the dissertation research" (p. 56). Roberts and Hyatt (2019) added,

> Since this chapter is written at the very end of the dissertation process, it may seem anticlimactic; however, in many ways, it is the dissertation's apex chapter. It provides answers to the problem stated in the introductory chapter and meaning to the research questions or hypotheses/null hypotheses in the methods chapter. This chapter is likely to be the one that researchers will read first, as readers typically turn to this chapter to get a whole sense of the research and the implications for the discipline. In other words, it is the *sine qua non*. (p. 173)

In certain ways, the discussion chapter should prove liberating. Whereas the researcher must practice strict adherence to the research questions, methods, analysis, and findings within chapters focused on these items, the discussion chapter affords researchers an opportunity to offer a degree of educated opinion and prioritization in regard to the implications of the findings and avenues for future research.

Most specifically, the final chapter of a dissertation should contain the following elements: an overview of the study; an interpretation of findings; limitations; implications for change; recommendations for action; recommendations for further study; and a conclusion. The aforementioned elements should be viewed as requisites, but other elements can be included.

Although there is seeming redundancy within a dissertation in that the purpose of the research, research questions, and the basic research approach are often mentioned in each chapter, this apparent redundancy serves a purpose. Readers often choose to read select chapters of a dissertation. As a result, the purpose of the research, research questions, and the basic research approach need to be front and center in individual chapters for ease of the reader. In particular, readers are attracted to the discussion chapter since it provides a summary of the findings, implications of those findings, and future avenues for research associated with the topic.

By the time researchers get to the final chapter of the dissertation or research project, they may feel a degree of weariness with both the topic and the research process. After all, the dissertation or manuscript serves as the culminating project of a degree or research project that involves a lot of work with what seems a myriad of items to track down and master. Even if a researcher is writing something other than a dissertation (e.g., journal article, technical report), there must be a discussion section that occurs at the end of a work. Rather than view the discussion section of a paper as the final task that must be accomplished, it would be far better to approach it with excitement. After all, the discussion portion of a manuscript is one's opportunity to interpret findings, make recommendations, and steer future research possibilities in a way that makes sense to the researcher. It is at the point of the discussion that the researcher becomes the expert. With this in mind, researchers should exhale after writing the discussion portion of a paper rather than prior to it.

OVERVIEW OF THE STUDY

Researchers should think of the overview of the study as an expanded abstract. This section should detail how the study was done, the research questions asked, and a summary of the findings. In other words, what was it that the researcher set out to do? Which questions were asked? Was the study qualitative, quantitative, or mixed methods? Was the study exploratory or explanatory? Were subjects involved, and if so, who were they? How were data collected and analyzed? In a general sense, what did the researcher discover? A reader of this section should be able to glean a good sense of what the research was about. An overview from Bradbury (2005) is found in textbox 6.1.

TEXTBOX 6.1.
Overview

This dissertation study was qualitative in nature, and it sought to discover the factors that contribute to both the academic success and lack of academic success of American Indian children at WOWE. Based on the findings of this study, the researcher made recommendations to the WOWE school board in regard to curricula, programming, policies, and procedures. The recommendations were made with the express purpose of improving academic achievement for students at WOWE, and specifically reducing the achievement gap between American Indian and White children. The researcher discovered that most of the gathered data were applicable to all children at WOWE, not American Indian children alone.

This study sought to answer four questions involving factors that affect student achievement. Through a qualitative approach and the use of focus groups as an instrument to gather data, the researcher asked the following questions:

1. What are the perceived factors that contribute to academic success of American Indian children at WOWE?
2. What are the perceived factors that inhibit student achievement among American Indian children at WOWE?

> 3. How do these perceived contributing and inhibiting factors influence student achievement at WOWE?
> 4. What curricula and programming would best serve the target population in terms of increased academic success?
>
> The researcher answered the first three questions through the use of categorized data. The fourth question is answered through the researcher's recommendations, which link directly to the categories.
>
> There was a total of six focus groups that contributed to the study, including a pilot project. The actual dissertation study involved five focus groups. They consisted of the following composition: 1) BST pass students; 2) BST non-pass students; 3) BST pass parents; 4) BST non-pass parents; and 5) teachers. The focus groups lasted about two hours and consisted of six participants on average. The focus groups produced approximately 270 pages of transcriptions.
>
> The researcher used a grounded theory approach, which involved open, axial, and selective coding. The researcher developed a theory through the coding and analysis of data. In addition, the researcher ensured valid findings through the use of triangulation; that is, corroboration between and among focus groups, and quantitative attitudinal and survey data.

In consideration of the components that should be present in an overview, the aforementioned excerpt answered the requisite questions as demonstrated below.

1. *What was it that the researcher set out to do?* "It sought to discover the factors that contribute to both the academic success and lack of academic success of American Indian children at WOWE" (p. 137).
2. *Which questions were asked?*

   - What are the perceived factors that contribute to academic success of American Indian children at WOWE?
   - What are the perceived factors that inhibit student achievement among American Indian children at WOWE?
   - How do these perceived contributing and inhibiting factors influence student achievement at WOWE?
   - What curricula and programming would best serve the target population in terms of increased academic success? (p. 137)

3. *Was the study qualitative, quantitative, or mixed methods?* Was the study exploratory or explanatory?

- "This dissertation study was qualitative in nature . . ." (p. 137)
- "It sought to discover the factors . . ." (p. 137)

4. *Were subjects involved, and if so, who were they?* There was a total of six focus groups that contributed to the study, including a pilot project. The actual dissertation study involved five focus groups. They consisted of the following composition: 1) BST pass students; 2) BST non-pass students; 3) BST pass parents; 4) BST non-pass parents; and 5) teachers. (p. 138)

5. *How were data collected and analyzed?* The researcher used a grounded theory approach, which involved open, axial, and selective coding. The researcher developed a theory through the coding and analysis of data. In addition, the researcher ensured valid findings through the use of triangulation; that is, corroboration between and among focus groups, and quantitative attitudinal and survey data. (p. 138)

6. *In a general sense, what did the researcher discover?* "The researcher developed a theory . . ." (p. 138)

INTERPRETATION OF FINDINGS

In reporting research findings, it is important to do so within the context of available literature. In other words, were findings consistent with those from the literature review utilized earlier in the paper? Were the findings contrary to those presented in the literature review? If so, how were the findings different than those reported in the literature review? Finally, were there any unexpected findings as the result of factors that influenced the overall methodological approach?

In consideration of the findings, as contextualized within available literature, several elements should be present to interpret fully the findings. These include:

1. Conclusions that address all of the research questions.
2. References to the outcomes of the findings.

3. Coverage of all reported data.
4. Adherence to the collected evidence.
5. Relating findings to a larger body of literature on the topic, including the conceptual/theoretical framework(s).
6. A discussion of the practical applications of the findings.

When reporting the conclusions of a study, the researcher must make certain to address all of the research questions. Some research may contain only one question or alternative/null hypothesis. Other research, however, may contain multiple research questions. Whether one question or multiple questions, conclusions associated with each research question must be listed.

In the discussion portion of one's paper, there must be a reference to the interpretation of the findings. In other words, what do the findings mean? The reader should not be left with a "So what?" attitude. It is the responsibility of the researcher to explain the various implications of the findings of the research. An example of the outcomes from Bradbury (2005) can be found in textbox 6.2.

Beyond these summary paragraphs that explain how the author arrived at the Theory of Low Standards (Expectations) through selective coding, Bradbury (2005, pp. 139–149) subsequently explained what the findings meant for each category and the relationship of those findings to the core standards category through axial coding.

One should keep in mind that conclusions and findings are not the same thing. As Roberts and Hyatt (2019) noted,

1. One conclusion may cut across more than one finding.
2. Don't confuse findings and conclusions. Findings are "the facts," whereas conclusions represent a higher level of abstraction—going beyond mere facts to higher levels of interpretation, analysis, and synthesis of findings. So, don't restate the research findings.
3. All conclusions must be backed up by your data and/or supported by the literature.
4. Don't add anything in this section not previously presented in the findings chapter.
5. This isn't the place for self-aggrandizing or exaggerated language, such as "The results of this study are important." If done carefully and properly, your study will stand on its own merit. (p. 177)

TEXTBOX 6.2.
Implications

Findings and Conclusions

Researcher's Theory of Low Standards

The researcher concluded that of the nine identified categories, the standards (expectations) category should serve as a core category. Although all nine categories and the respective properties were important, the remaining eight categories, which were titled role modeling and support systems, societal influences, teacher quality and effectiveness, relevancy of education, communication and recognition, ethnicity, involvement, and school environment, all tied to the standards category in some way. As a result, the researcher theorizes that the fundamental reason for a lack of achievement on the part of American Indian students at WOWE is lowered standards on the part of students, parents, teachers, administration, and society. In other words, American Indian children at WOWE underachieve because those with a vested interest in their education have simply lowered standards to a point that underachievement is more likely than not.

The theory of lowered standards is supported by gathered data that were categorized. The bottom line is that lowered expectations lead to decreased academic performance as misbehavior, absence of decorum, and decreased academic rigor are accepted and in some cases promoted through poor role modeling and a compromised learning environment.

LIMITATIONS OF THE STUDY

All studies have limitations, and these limitations may be mentioned in more than one place in a dissertation study or paper. In addition, both limitations and delimitations may be addressed within the same section of a paper. However, keep in mind that there are differences between limitations and delimitations. Limitations are influences that the researcher cannot control, and delimitations are choices or parameters chosen by the researcher. However, limitations should be included in the discussion portion of the paper. Kristjansson-Nelson (2020a) explained the limitations of her study, found in textbox 6.3.

TEXTBOX 6.3.
Implications

Limitations and Delimitations

Data collection for the study took place over a 10-day period of time, in and around Sydney, Australia, where interviews, observations, and focus groups were conducted at two different sites run by Bus Stop Films. As previously noted, one limitation of the study is the generalizability. Given the delimited scope of data collection from one non-profit media arts education organization, the findings will not be generalizable to other media arts or film production education organizations. Generalizability was not a priority for this study, as there was greater emphasis placed on gaining insight from the experiences of students, staff, teachers, and administrators at this particular organization.

As noted, the study was delimited to one non-profit media arts education organization, Bus Stop Films. Thus, an additional delimitation can be found in the range of media arts taught by the organization. Though Bus Stop Films teaches a range of media arts disciplines, including animation and VR, as well as components of all media arts disciplines, film production is by far the primary focus of the organization's curriculum. Thus, the findings are limited to the area of film production and cannot necessarily be generalized to all media arts disciplines.

Like many studies, the research was limited by time, money, and scheduling logistics. Had limitations not been a factor, the study could have been strengthened by multiple site visits over time, in order to engage with participants in a manner that would have allowed for data collection and data analysis, followed by more data collection and more data analysis, and so on. Given the significant geographic distance between the researcher and the participants, additional site visits were not feasible. Though it is the position of the researcher that saturation occurred, the findings lead to the desire for more research, which will be discussed in the recommendations section of this chapter.

In the case of the aforementioned study (Kristjansson-Nelson, 2020a), delimitations included two sites. However, the location of those sites, combined with resource considerations, generated a number of limitations. All research must have a limited scope; that is, boundaries or parameters that should be viewed as delimitations. Once delimitations are set, factors outside the control of the researcher should be viewed as limitations.

IMPLICATIONS FOR CHANGE

In writing a discussion of one's findings, there must be a "so what" section. In other words, the researcher needs to explain why the findings are important. However, what must be understood when writing this section of the paper is that nothing revolutionary needs to be reported; that is, the research findings may confirm what is already in the literature. The researcher should not be disappointed if nothing "new" was discovered as the result of the study. Corroboration with or departure from findings previously reported in research is perfectly fine. Reaching similar or different conclusions as those already present in the literature should be understood as valuable.

The value in research, whether it corroborates or disputes findings from previous studies, is what the findings mean for purposes of implications. As Roberts and Hyatt (2019) explained,

> Your research findings have implications that are discipline-specific for other scholars. This is one of the areas where a thorough review of the literature reflects your expertise in the subject and affords you the opportunity to indicate how the findings of your study add to the body of literature on the subject. (p. 177)

One misunderstanding that beginning scholars tend to have is that of the need to discover something not already found in the literature. While it is certain that some studies will help to fill holes in the literature on a specific topic, many studies will contribute to the literature in more subtle ways.

RECOMMENDATIONS FOR ACTION

An essential part of the discussion portion of the paper involves recommendations. While the discussion will include recommendations for further study, as noted in the next section, recommendations for action are essential. While findings are often interesting in and of themselves, it is important for the researcher to make recommendations that either substantiate the status quo or call for change.

Before making recommendations, the researcher should think about the alternative/null hypotheses and/or the research questions and the findings associated with the hypotheses or questions. These questions should be restated just prior to the recommendations so as to provide easy reference for the reader. Prior to listing recommendations, Bradbury (2005) provided a reminder of the research questions.

1. What are the perceived factors that contribute to academic success of American Indian children at WOWE?
2. What are the perceived factors that inhibit student achievement among American Indian children at WOWE?
3. How do these perceived contributing and inhibiting factors influence student achievement among American Indian children at WOWE?
4. What curricula and programming would best serve the target population in terms of increased academic success? (p. 137)

In writing recommendations, it is important to provide a reasonable degree of specificity. Vague recommendations leave far too much room for interpretation and hold little promise for implementation. Bradbury (2005, pp. 150–158) provided 45 recommendations for implementation within a school district, including those found in textbox 6.4.

In consideration of these sample recommendations, the specificity should be apparent. For example, instead of leaving a recommendation vague, such as "WOWE needs to do a better job of communicating with parents," Bradbury (2005, p. 156) detailed the types and frequency of communication and the responsible parties.

TEXTBOX 6.4.
Recommendations

- Students who disrupt the classroom and refuse to work need to be placed in an alternative educational setting until they can demonstrate enough maturity to function in mainstream educational classes. Prior to short-term placement in this setting, the teacher should implement a series of interventions, including a conference with the student, parent, and administrator. Students who fail to succeed in this setting should be referred to long-term alternative educational settings or review for special education services. (p. 150)
- Teachers need to be organized and prepared. All teachers should be required to develop syllabuses for each class or grade level they teach. In addition, lesson plans should tie directly to the syllabus, and they should be detailed. (p. 154)
- Teachers should subscribe to the direct model of instruction. This model sets forth the daily objectives, gets the attention of students, involves the teaching of a new skill, and allows time for guided and independent practice of the new skill. Lessons should be varied and should accommodate all modalities, including opportunities for tactile learners. Many American Indian children prefer group activities that provide tactile opportunities. Teachers should vary their lesson plans so that no activity is more than 15 minutes in length, unless the nature of the class is almost exclusively hands-on and dictates otherwise. (p. 154)
- WOWE needs to do a better job of communicating with parents. WOWE should implement a directive whereby all elementary teachers make contact with parents via telephone, email, or letter a minimum of one time per month. Secondary teachers should be required to contact the parents of their students a minimum of one time per quarter. This contact should be above and beyond mid-term reporting and report cards. When contact is made, there should be some positive comments expressed.

RECOMMENDATIONS FOR FURTHER STUDY

Although not necessarily lengthy in number or verbiage, the researcher should include recommendations for further study. Roberts and Hyatt (2019) noted,

> You are expected to present recommendations for ways the topic of your study can be advanced and how future studies might contribute to the field. These recommendations may arise from constraints imposed on your study, such as conditions you could not or chose not to control. The recommendations can also stem from the study limitations. Some examples of limitations include population and sample, study size, methodology, environment, geography, policy, and when the study was conducted. (pp. 177–178)

The bottom line is that recommendations for further study can stem from various aspects of one's research. Burklund (2020) made this clear by noting recommendations stemming from his study (see textbox 6.5).

TEXTBOX 6.5.
Recommendations for Future Research

Recommendations for Future Studies

There are a great number of future studies that the researcher envisions as the next steps to the study. First and foremost, while the volume of survey responses for this study offered a robust opportunity to analyze satisfaction, the results were not collected under a controlled environment. One of the focus group participants noted that they tend to only fill out the surveys when they have something positive or negative to say about their experience. As such, the researcher would like to see a controlled study with participants randomly divided into groups to attend training in different modalities. A future study could include the development and deployment of a more detailed questionnaire specific to the study and specific to the constructs of synchronous online fashion.

Additionally, the researcher believes there could be great value in expanding the qualitative analysis for understanding satisfaction by reviewing the free-form fields submitted on the Level-1 surveys. The researcher had 147,315 individual comments that were pulled along with the four years' worth of survey results. These comments offer a robust opportunity to further explore satisfaction by modality.

Finally, the corporate and education worlds do differ in the types of learners and content that is delivered. However, at the core, there are a lot of opportunities they are synergistic. Many of the learners from the traditional education institutions move on to join workforce is that incorporate various elements of learning and development within training. To better gauge how the formulation of factors influencing satisfaction, a future study comparing synchronous online satisfaction between different populations of learners could indicate if the synergy should be closer or more contrasted between educational practices.

RESEARCHER'S REFLECTION

Prior to the conclusion of the study, a researcher may choose to add an optional section that involves the reflections of a researcher. This reflection, in particular, may be appropriate for qualitative studies. This reflection may include the researcher's experience with the research process in which the researcher discusses possible personal biases or preconceived ideas and values, the possible effects of the researcher on the participants or the situation, and changes in thinking as a result of the study.

CONCLUSION

All research papers need a conclusion. This conclusion is not a detailed examination of all that was shared in the paper. Instead, the conclusion is an opportunity to impress on the reader the major points that are key to the paper. In all likelihood, these points should include major findings and implications for either the specific subject of the research or more generalized implications, if appropriate. When readers finish the paper, they should be able to know what was truly important about the study and why the author knows that to be the case. Kristjansson-Nelson (2020a) made clear the most important take-aways in the final paragraph of her dissertation, as found in textbox 6.6. As the researcher, it is critical to leave the reader with a lasting impression of "what" is important and why the "what" is important.

TEXTBOX 6.6.
Conclusion

Having identified dispositions as an active catalyst within leadership practices and filmmaking practices, film and media arts educators may wish
to examine programmatic standards for professional practice, as well as
pedagogical practices that prioritize aspects of collaboration and inclusion
over product and *the amateur*. Working toward such changes will place
greater emphasis on the need for an inclusive culture, in which all voices
can participate without the interference of attitudinal barriers.

7

QUALITATIVE RESEARCH DESIGNS

A challenging aspect of research involves terminology, and the term *research design* is no exception. Some researchers tend to use certain terms (e.g., *conceptual* and *theoretical frameworks*) synonymously. The terms *strategy*, *approach*, *perspective*, and *methodology* are used by some researchers in lieu of *design*. For those trying to understand research, it is important to keep in mind that although terminology may vary, research design is critical to the integrity of a research inquiry.

Research design involves one's chosen paradigm, ontological beliefs, and epistemological views. In a nutshell, research design refers to the overall strategy or approach that one utilizes to accomplish research, replete with research questions, methods for data collection, data analysis, and interpretation of results. Scott (2012, p. 107) referred to research design as "the means by which the objectives or aims of the study are fulfilled." In layperson's terms, ontology refers to knowledge or reality, and epistemology refers to the means by which one knows reality. Ontological and epistemological viewpoints cannot be separated from one's paradigm since paradigms determine whether there are singular or varying truths. If one were to subscribe to the paradigm of positivism, for example, one would believe in a singular truth about reality (ontology) that can be objectively measured with reliable and valid tools. On the other hand, one who subscribes to the paradigm of subjectivism would believe that reality is a matter of perspective (ontology) and truth is whatever one perceives (epistemology) it to be. Only certain methods are appropriate for certain paradigm/ontology/epistemology combinations, and as a result, one's research design must be a holistic view of a project so as to provide the necessary research components (e.g., methods, analysis, and interpretation) to answer the research questions that are asked. Denzin and Lincoln (2000) alluded to the paradigmatic, ontological, and epistemological connection by noting,

> Five basic questions structure the issue of design: (a) How will the design connect to the paradigm or perspective being used? That is, how will empirical materials be informed by and interact with the paradigm in question? (b) How will these materials allow the researcher to speak to the problems of praxis and change? (c) Who or what will be studied? (d) What strategies of inquiry will be used? (e) What methods or research tools will be used for collecting and analyzing empirical materials? (p. 368)

Greater detail regarding paradigms, ontology, epistemology, and research perspectives was provided in Chapter 1, but in the broadest of ways, researchers must choose quantitative, qualitative, or mixed methods research design. Each line of inquiry, whether quantitative, qualitative, or mixed methods, lends itself better to certain paradigms, ontologies, and epistemologies. This chapter explains major qualitative research designs and associated data analyses with the understanding that mixed methods inquiry requires the incorporation of elements of both qualitative and quantitative research.

QUALITATIVE RESEARCH DESIGNS

Although qualitative research designs are greater in number than five, this section delimits qualitative research design as follows: ethnography; narrative; phenomenology; grounded theory; and case study. These research designs were chosen since they are utilized with frequency within qualitative inquiry. It should be remembered that research design is the glue that holds together research questions and the collection and analysis of data. Moreover, Gray (2018), in commenting on approaches to qualitative design, noted,

> It is strongly influenced by the epistemological stance adopted by the researcher. A further, and connected, influence will occur if the researcher is an adherent of any of the qualitative strategies. For example, adherents of the ethnographic school will, obviously, adopt ethnographic design methods, usually involving observation and participation. It is important, however, to distinguish between qualitative data gathering methods (such as observation or focus groups) and the holistic framework of a research design. Data gathering methods are incorporated, and are sometimes intrinsically associated, with a particular design. Observation, for example, is often associated with ethnographic research design. For other qualitative research designs, such as case studies or grounded theory, a wide variety of data gathering instruments are valid. (p. 169)

What must be kept in mind is that research design is holistic and all-encompassing of one's research rather than a particular part of it.

Ethnography

Ethnography, which has been most closely associated with the discipline of anthropology in the past, involves the immersion of oneself into a particular group, culture, or community as an observer, and at the heart of ethnography is the idea of detailed observation of social interaction among those in that particular group, culture, or community. Tedlock (2000) explained,

> Ethnography involves an ongoing attempt to place specific encounters, events, and understandings into a fuller, more meaningful context. It is not simply the production of new information or research data but rather the way in which such information or data are transformed into a written or visual form. As a result, it combines research design, fieldwork, and various methods of inquiry to produce historically, politically, and personally situated accounts, descriptions, interpretations, and representations of human lives. (p. 455)

Ethnography allows the researcher to get a detailed sense of what is happening within a particular group of people relative to setting and social interaction. As Nagy Hesse-Biber and Leavy (2011, p. 193) noted, "Ethnographic research aims to get a holistic understanding of how individuals in different cultures and subcultures make sense of their lived reality." By going inside the world of the target population, the researcher can gain the necessary insight to understand the dynamics of group interaction, which results in a thick and detailed description of everyday life.

Since ethnography requires both immersion and a commitment of time in the field, this research design may prove more problematic for those who are faced with items (e.g., work, family) that vie for one's time. With this noted, there are more modest approaches to ethnographic research. Gray (2018) explained,

> Ethnography seeks to understand social processes less by making reports of these events (for example, through using an interview) than by participating within them, often for long periods of time. Overt or covert participant observation, then, would be a typical approach to data collection in ethnographic research. While ethnography generally involves "immersion" in the field for long periods, micro-ethnography adopts a more focused approach on, say, one aspect or element of work or social setting, allowing for observation over a few weeks or months. (pp. 166–167)

Ethnography relies upon interpretation rather than a singular truth. Nagy Hesse-Biber and Leavy (2011, p. 198) reminded researchers that an ethnographic work relies on "an interpretative rather than a positivist perspective on the nature of reality." In other words, as stressed earlier in this chapter, one's paradigm and epistemological beliefs matter when it comes to research. If one disagrees ontologically that truth is influenced by perspective, then ethnography would not be the correct research design choice. One caveat associated with an interpretative approach, however, is provided by Mason (2018, p. 133), who submitted, "A major challenge for interpretivist approaches centres on the question of how you can be sure and demonstrate to others that you are not simply inventing data or misrepresenting your research participants' perspectives." Certain research practices can be utilized to provide assurances that ethnographic results are trustworthy. The means to address the challenge associated with an interpretivist approach will be covered later in this chapter.

An example of ethnographic research can be found in the autoethnographical account of travel in post-apartheid South Africa, as shared by Bradbury (2011b), who noted that the purpose of his autoethnographical account was to provide a Midwesterner's experience in the bush in post-apartheid South Africa. More specifically, Bradbury (para. 1) "strove to make sense of the sociocultural context in which he found himself by observing the interplay between Africans and Whites over the course of two safaris, and by recalling personal stories and examining his own belief systems as the result of his upbringing."

Narrative Inquiry

Narrative inquiry is a somewhat sweeping term in that it encompasses one's life story through singular or multiple methods. With a narrative research design, the research idea is one of storytelling. More specifically, Constable et al. (n.d., para. 1) defined narrative inquiry as "the process of gathering information for the purpose of research through storytelling." Narrative research may involve either biographical or autobiographical accounts. Gray (2018) explained narrative analysis and biographical research in the following way:

> Narrative analysis is the analysis of a chronologically told story, with a focus on how the various elements of the story are sequenced. Key elements in narrative analysis include "scripts," predictive frames that people use to determine events, and stories that expand on scripts, adding evaluative elements that reveal the narrator's viewpoints. Narrative analysis tends to use the narrative interview as the primary method of data collection, with a focus on the biographical experiences of the respondent. The research focus of narrative analysis often includes issues that deal with ethical, moral and cultural ambiguities. (p. 168)

An example of narrative inquiry is found in the dissertation research of Cirks (2021, see textbox 7.1).

TEXTBOX 7.1.
Narrative Inquiry

The primary purpose of this qualitative study is to gain an understanding of the experiences that impact American Indian students' non-persistence and persistence in pursuing advanced degrees. In the end, with the literature review and this qualitative study, it will be more apparent why graduate school is the road less traveled by many American Indian students. (p. 34)

Phenomenology

With phenomenology, there is no singular reality. Instead, truth is in the eyes of the beholder. In other words, the reactions, perceptions, and feelings of individuals are of great importance, not the researcher's viewpoint. Gray (2018) reinforced these points by noting,

> Phenomenologists argue that the relation between perception and objects is not passive—human consciousness actively constructs the world as well as perceiving it. Phenomenological ideas were first applied to social sciences research by the German philosopher Alfred Shutz (1899–1959), who argued that social reality has a specific meaning and relevance structure for people who are living, thinking and experiencing it. And, it is these thought structures (objects) that determine their behavior by motivating it. It also follows that the thought objects constructed by researchers who are trying to grasp reality, have to be founded upon the thought objects of ordinary men and women living their daily lives in the social world. It is necessary, then, for researchers to gain access to people's common-sense thinking in order to interpret and understand their actions. In other words, phenomenology seeks to understand the world from the participant's point of view. This can only be achieved if the researcher "brackets out" their own preconceptions. (p. 167)

As a researcher, phenomenology affords significant latitude in what reality is, but it comes with the precondition that reality is relative to the experiences, feelings, and perceptions of the research participants, not the researcher. With this noted, a researcher would likely subscribe to the paradigm of constructivism/interpretivism and the ontological and epistemological beliefs, respectively, that there is no single reality, and realities must be interpreted to have meaning.

When choosing an appropriate research design, even if the researcher has settled upon qualitative research, it is important to consider the pros and cons of qualitative research designs. Dass (2020) articulated his rationale for choosing phenomenology over case study design as seen in textbox 7.2.

TEXTBOX 7.2.
Research Design Rationale

A case study design was not selected for the study due to the fundamental differences in design structure. Similar to other qualitative research designs, case studies entrench researchers into very particular situations in which they explore phenomena or within a real-life, contemporary context (Yin, 2014). This study seeks to discern the broader phenomena driving a particular dynamic within a particular context, theoretical framework, and with a pool of like participants. This study design matches poorly with a case study design, in that not one particular event, events specific to a particular constituency, or profiled. Thus, the decision was made to facilitate a study anchored by a phenomenological research design.

Grounded Theory

Grounded theory owes its start to Glaser and Strauss (1967), and it has been influential in qualitative research design in that it is both inductive and systematic. Simply put, grounded theory rejects a priori theorizing. As opposed to a deductive approach, which would start with a preconception or hypothesis that is applied to particular participants or settings, grounded theory utilizes an inductive approach of broad themes to generate a specific theory. Unlike quantitative approaches that strive to disprove the null hypothesis so as to prove the alternative hypothesis, grounded theory allows themes to emerge from data via coding, which results in theory generation. The researcher utilizes a systematic approach when analyzing data to establish categories, themes, and theory through open, axial, and selective coding. Kristjansson-Nelson (2020a) articulated grounded theory methodology in her dissertation (see textbox 7.3). As with Bockelmann (2021) and Dass (2020), Kristjansson-Nelson (2020a) provided rationale for selecting the qualitative research design that she chose relative to other designs (see textbox 7.4).

TEXTBOX 7.3.
Grounded Theory Description

Grounded Theory

Grounded theory is a qualitative approach that offers researchers a means to generate new theories that can aid the progress of many disciplines. "Grounded theory is a research approach and methodology, employing a combination of inductive and deductive methods, following within the interpretive paradigm, relying on conventional qualitative methods of data collection and a unique system of coding in data analysis" (Dimmock & Lam, 2012, p. 188). Grounded theory has its roots in naturalistic inquiry, which breaks from positivism with a multidimensional ontology, dismissing the notion that there is only one reality.

TEXTBOX 7.4.
Research Design Rationale Relative to Other Designs

Grounded theory, like naturalistic inquiry, seeks to more deeply understand human experiences through purposive sampling. "The aim is not to find a representative case from which to generalize findings . . . [but rather] to develop interpretations and local theories that afford deep insights into the human experience" (Armstrong, 2010, p. 880). Rather than focusing on a person's story through narrative research or shared experiences through phenomenology, grounded theory aims to generate a theory that "might help explain practice or provide a framework for further research" (Creswell & Poth, 2018, p. 82). To that end, grounded theory "is well suited to studies in education leadership . . . because of its availability to offer a theory or explanation of complex interactive situations involving human beings in their natural or organizational settings" (Dimmock & Lam, 2012, p. 189).

Case Study

A case study is an in-depth analysis of something (e.g., people, events, and relationships) tied together by some common feature. According to Simons (2009, p. 21), "case study is an in-depth exploration from multiple perspectives of the complexity and uniqueness of a particular project, policy, institution, programme or system in a 'real-life' context." Nagy Hesse-Biber and Leavy (2018) added,

> The unique contribution of a case study approach is that it provides the researcher with a holistic understanding of a problem, issue, or phenomenon within its social context. Cases can be individuals, events, programs, institutions, or a society. Case study research usually relies on one or a few cases to investigate (typically, one case for which ample multidimensional data is [sic] collected and analyzed. (p. 256)

Bockelmann (2021) understood clearly the contribution of case study research design as seen in textbox 7.5. As with Dass (2020) and Kristjansson-Nelson (2020a), Bockelmann (2021) was clear as to why she chose case study over phenomenology or grounded theory as seen in textbox 7.6.

TEXTBOX 7.5.
Contribution of Case Study Research Design

The purpose of this study was to expose the ways in which teacher leadership was viewed by different stakeholders within an organization and reflect upon the outcomes regarding teacher practice. This study added to the knowledge base of organizational leadership in education by examining teacher leadership from a systemic standpoint, the pragmatic standpoint of teachers, and patterns of behavior between the roles of teacher, teacher leaders, and principals.

TEXTBOX 7.6.
Case Study Rationale

A phenomenological approach would not have been appropriate as this study consists of two parts and draws conclusions between them as a lens for systemic improvement. Though both phenomenology and case study require a recount of the lived experiences of participants, one single phenomenon is not being studied as in phenomenology; rather, a system was studied (Creswell & Poth, 2018; Merriam & Tisdell, 2016, p. 37; Yazan, 2015). A grounded theory approach might have been used if a hypothesis did not already exist and a specific phenomenon pinpointed to illuminate. Surveys could also have been used to garner quantitative data regarding the perspectives of the participants, however the rich descriptions of the situation and reasons behind the responses of the participants that are needed to answer the complex research questions would be missed (Creswell & Poth, 2018).

QUALITATIVE DATA ANALYSIS

The Influence of Research Design

Research design refers to the overall approach that a researcher utilizes. Research design includes the integration of the various components of the research in an intelligible and coherent manner to ensure that the research questions are addressed in proper fashion. Research design constitutes the study blueprint, replete with choices regarding data collection processes, methods, and analysis. Those familiar with research tend to argue that research questions drive the research design, and in large part, this would be true. However, in all likelihood, researchers would be most interested in asking questions representative of those that would lend themselves to a preferred paradigm and ontological and epistemological beliefs. For example, one who subscribes to the paradigm of constructivism/interpretivism would not, in all likelihood, try to disprove a null hypothesis to show cause and effect of variables. Instead, researchers who view themselves as constructivists/interpretivists would ask research questions that would allow for multiple truths through interpretation of data.

Purpose of Research to Determine Data Analysis

Part of a research design, and one that can prove problematic for beginning researchers, involves the purpose of one's research project. According to Gray (2018), the purpose of a research project may be exploratory, descriptive, explanatory, or interpretive.

Exploratory Studies

Exploratory studies, as the name would suggest, are concerned with the exploration of a topic. Exploratory studies don't attempt to explain phenomena, but rather explore the worthiness of future research within a topic area. Exploratory studies can be useful in generating ideas as to why certain phenomena may be, and as a result, exploratory studies can prove fertile ground for future research. It should be understood, however, that exploratory studies do not provide an explanation.

Descriptive Studies

As suggested by their name, descriptive studies describe the state of something. Descriptive studies can help to explain who, what, and where, but not why. For example, a descriptive study could examine test score results of students against various demographic classifications to determine who performs best on a criterion- or norm-referenced exam and factors that could be associated with the demographic groups, but the study wouldn't explain why disparities exist. Descriptive studies can help to connect dots among related items of a particular topic or area of study.

Explanatory Studies

As with exploratory and descriptive studies, explanatory studies are aptly named. Explanatory studies explain the connection between phenomena or variables that would be present in descriptive studies. Whereas descriptive studies explain who, what, or where, explanatory studies explain why. Beginning researchers sometimes want to show cause and effect or provide the why associated with a topic of interest. While humans tend to be curious and want to know why certain things are, researchers will find that there is more latitude with exploratory studies than one finds with explanatory studies since exploratory studies are not designed to show causal connections.

Interpretive Studies

Interpretive studies explore the lives of people, their experiences, viewpoints, and perspectives. Gray (2018, p. 37) noted that "interpretive studies are, typically, inductive in nature and often associated with qualitative approaches to data gathering and analysis." As with exploratory studies, interpretive studies afford researchers greater flexibility.

Thematic Analysis and Coding

In qualitative research, regardless of the paradigm to which one subscribes, a common way of analyzing data involves thematic analysis through coding. Coding is to qualitative research what the heartbeat is to the human body. Coding pumps life into one's qualitative data since it is through coding that data are analyzed. Without data analysis and subsequent interpretation, qualitative inquiry should not be called research. Fielding (2002) noted,

> Coding is fundamental to qualitative data analysis. The corpus has to be divided into segments and these segments assigned codes . . . which relate to the analytic themes being developed. Researchers aim for codes which capture some essential quality of the segment, and which apply to other segments too. (p. 163)

Coding can take many shapes and forms, it can be deductive or inductive, and it can involve basic theme to theory generation. There are some basic rules to coding, and these involve an organized way by which the author labels or tags small pieces of data for future use when aggregated with other small pieces of data. The systematic or organized way in which data are coded and analyzed should begin with basic coding. Consider basic coding to be the view from 10,000 feet. One can pick out the obvious things, but closer inspection is necessary to get a more granular and revealing view. Punch (2011) reinforced this idea by making clear that basic coding is the first step in data analysis.

Basic thematic coding can take various forms, and the coding approach may be called by various names. For example, Larson (2020) utilized the Data Analysis Spiral Method (Creswell & Poth, 2018; see textbox 7.7), which involved approaching the data by means of analytical circles rather than a linear approach. Another example of coding utilized by Burklund (2020) involved both deductive coding (a priori codes) and open and axial coding (see textboxes 7.8 and 7.9).

TEXTBOX 7.7.
Data Analysis Spiral Method

With this type of coding, data were organized and managed, and the researcher read the data and noted emerging ideas in the margins of the focus group transcript. The notes consisted of thoughts, ideas, observations, and questions that stood out to the researcher as being of interest to her research questions. Next, the commentary of the researcher along with the participant narrative began to take shape in the form of codes. These primary codes represented key items pulled from the focus group discussion. Once the primary codes were established, it was important to categorize the codes into a broader context. As these categories were created, the researcher aligned each individual code under these broader secondary codes. As the categorization phase ended, the final codes were then analyzed and interpreted even more broadly as themes. The resulting themes and codes were then put into a table format with their respective qualitative supporting data in the Virtual Focus Group Code Book (see Appendix I). The spiraled analysis was concluded with a representation and/or visualization of the data (Creswell & Poth, 2018). This visual representation will be presented in Chapter 4. Upon completion of the analysis, the data from this focus group were combined with quantitative results for a final analysis and interpretation that is discussed in Chapter 5.

TEXTBOX 7.8.
Deductive Coding (A Priori Codes)
and Open and Axial Coding, Part I

The deductive coding model was selected by the researcher to help provide guidance during the data analysis phase. Using available research and frameworks, the researcher was able to create a rough codebook of potential factors/themes expected to be present during the focus groups.

However, the codebook utilized by the researcher simply served as a starting point in the data analysis process and evolved and changed after all focus groups had concluded. A starting codebook was based on the TIPEC conceptual framework created by Ali, Saman, and Uppal (2018). An exhaustive review, spanning nearly 30 years of research, uncovered 68 barriers of why e-learning often fails compared to traditional learning. They named their framework based upon the four thematic groups that emerged: "Technology (T), Individual (I), Pedagogy (P), and Enabling Conditions (EC)" (Ali, Saman, & Uppal, 2018, p. 156). A copy of the TIPEC framework can be found in Appendix H and the final codebook is included in Appendix I.

TEXTBOX 7.9.
Deductive Coding (A Priori Codes) and Open and Axial Coding, Part 2

After the focus group interviews were completed, information gathered from the recordings was synthesized and analyzed. The researcher opted to use a blend of both deductive and inductive coding methods to analyze the results of the focus group. Since few studies have produced guidelines for satisfaction in synchronous online environments, the researcher utilized the Tipec Framework (see Appendix H) as a guide for potential themes. The Tipec Framework is geared more toward asynchronous online classrooms so the researcher also utilized an open coding to search for themes outside of the Tipec Framework and axial process to categorize and connect all of the emergent themes to develop an overall understanding of satisfaction. Open coding was used to "generate concepts," whereas axial coding "was used to make connections among the categories and their sub-categories, as identified in the open-coding stage" (Briggs, Coleman, & Morrison, 2012, p. 198). Following the convergent mixed-methods approach, quantitative data and themes/trends from the Level-1 surveys were compared in tandem with the outcomes of the focus groups and research. Themes and trends from the focus groups were synthesized with the sub-categories of the Level-1 to check for alignment. For example, a theme from the focus group citing lower satisfaction with synchronous online because of social interaction might be connected to a question in the Level-1 survey regarding engagement. Additionally, data from the literature review were synthesized to help explain the results. The final results of the converged data provided an outlet to understand differences in satisfaction between synchronous online and face-to-face classrooms as well as the specific factors influencing satisfaction the most.

One should keep in mind that deductive coding involves the use of a priori codes and inductive coding utilizes emergent codes. With deductive coding, the use of a priori codes means that the researcher has set words or phrases, and the utilization of open coding allows the researcher to look for those words or phrases. In the case of Burklund (2020, p. 139), he looked for the terms *technology, individual, pedagogy,* and *enabling conditions* within the TIPIC Framework during the initial (open) coding process. During the axial coding process, Burklund looked for connections among these categories to establish themes. Another researcher, Ades (2020), utilized both deductive and inductive coding to analyze his data (see textbox 7.10).

TEXTBOX 7.10.
Deductive and Inductive Coding

The andragogical assumptions regarding adult learners that guided data collection translated into a priori codes in the analysis process. Deductive coding utilized predetermined codes gleaned from the literature review. This type of coding is a top-down approach, where the researcher brings a set of significant perceptions to the data. These being self-directedness, previous experience, life relevant, problem/solution oriented and intrinsic motivation. Under the theme of andragogical characteristics, these deductive codes were sought in the data.

Creswell (2018) warned, "If a prefigured coding scheme is used in analysis, we typically encourage the researchers to be open to additional codes emerging during the analysis" (p. 193). Inductive coding is a bottom-up approach. This type of coding allows the data to suggest their own significant perceptions without the researcher's predetermination. Following this guidance, a set of inductive codes emerged utilizing an interpretive, constant comparative approach. This process involved repetitively going through the data in order to identify similarities and differences. Multiple readings of the collected data produced preliminary codes evolving into final constructs categorizing the data. These emerged themes described the meaning participants had assigned to their experience. Thomas (2016) summarized, "The basic principle governing the process of constant comparison is that you emerge with themes that capture or summarise the essence (or essences) of your data" (p. 205). Both deductive and inductive coding were utilized within this analysis.

The deductive and inductive coding, as presented by Ades (2020) from one of his research sites, resulted in table 7.1. This table is illustrative of the simple end to a rather time-consuming process. What is important is that the researcher selects a process of coding that makes sense and fits the situation.

Table 7.1. Site Four Analysis.

Theme	Deductive Coding	Text Evidence Sample
Andragogical characteristics	Self-directedness	They are basically telling us what to do to help them get done. (P) . . . it ends up that they are very independent and they can manage themselves very well. (N) . . . students feel confident and feel empowered that they have control over their own education. (E)
	Life relevant	You get students to an endpoint that is much more relevant to them. (P) Relevancy for our students is to be able to effectively help their children become better scholars. (E) We are doing this to get the skill competency done, you're getting more skill that you can take back to work. (P)
	Intrinsic motivation	They get into these little cohorts that motivate them to keep going. (M) And then there are those people who are motivated super intrinsically or by personal reasons. (M). I will say though on a bigger scale once we get students into the program I think the adult diploma has some built-in motivators. (E)

Theme	Inductive Coding	Text evidence sample
Empowerment	Equity	We talk about equity all the time; that is equity. (T) That is really what I think about when I think about equity. (E) That is part of what equity is; it's not equality. (P)
	Advocacy	And very much advocating for what they need. (T) And you have the tools you need to advocate for what you need to succeed. (P) Advocating for their child's learning, that is very powerful. (P)

Source: Ades (2020, p. 99).

While the coding by Larson (2020), Burklund (2020), and Ades (2020) did not lead to theory generation, the work by Kristjansson-Nelson (2020a) resulted in theory production via a grounded theory approach. If one wants to generate a theory, as opposed to generating themes only, then the grounded theory approach must be utilized with qualitative research. The grounded theory approach utilizes open, axial, and selective coding, which involves categorization, connection of categories, and the selection of core categories to generate theory (Gray, 2000, pp. 694–700). Kristjansson-Nelson's explanation of her rationale and systematic process of open, axial, and selective coding is found in textboxes 7.11 and 7.12.

TEXTBOX 7.11.
Rationale of Open, Axial, and Selective Coding

For example, the Glaserian approach calls for two levels of coding, whereas the Straussian approach calls for three. The first level of coding in the Glaserian approach is referred to as substantive coding, whereas the Straussian approach begins with open coding (Heath & Cowley, 2004, p. 146). The Straussian approach then "involves two further types of coding, each representing a successively higher level of abstraction; these are axial and selective coding . . . both are based on exploring the relationships and interrelationships between categories" (Dimmock & Lam, 2012, p. 197). Because of the variation between the 65 Glaserian and Straussian approaches to the process, there are "two issues . . . the role of induction, and emergence vs. deduction and speculation" (Heath & Cowley, 2004, p. 143). Glaser believed Straussian grounded theory shouldn't use a "deductive emphasis, which requires the asking of numerous questions and speculation about what might be rather than what exists in the data" (Heath & Cowley, 2004, p. 144). However, due to the systematic design and specific coding steps, Strauss and Corbin's process is likely a stronger choice for researchers new to grounded theory methods.

TEXTBOX 7.12.
Process of Open, Axial, and Selective Coding

Once data were collected and transcribed to text, data analysis began. In keeping with the Straussian approach to grounded theory (Strauss & Corbin, 1998), open, axial, and selective coding was used to draw out themes from the data. The process began with open coding, through which "data are broken down into discrete parts, closely examined, and compared for similarities and differences" (Strauss & Corbin, 1998, p. 102). Microanalysis is key to the process, which the authors described as a "minute examination and interpretation 83 of data" (p. 58). Open coding and microanalysis required close attention to detail in the data, looking at words and phrases, and carefully listening. That process facilitated codes and themes to be identified, as a central phenomenon emerged from the collected data. The study then followed Strauss & Corbin's (1998) procedures for asking questions and making comparisons in order to inform theoretical sampling as needed. Conceptualizing was central to the process, as memos were used, and labels were attached to phenomena found within the data.

After labels were created for this study's data, classification began in order to group concepts into categories, which is the process of axial coding. "The purpose of axial coding is to begin the process of reassembling data that were fractured during open coding" (Strauss & Corbin, 1998, p. 124). As the authors noted, data analysis between the steps of open and axial coding are not sequential, and thus analysis for this study moved freely between these types of coding throughout the data analysis process.

In moving toward the development of a theory, selective coding was used. "Selective coding is the process of integrating and refining categories" (Strauss & Corbin, 1998, p. 143). A central category was identified as one to which all other categories could be related, and integration was then facilitated by some of the techniques outlined by the authors (i.e., writing a story and drawing diagrams).

CONCLUSION

All of the aforementioned examples of coding from actual research projects were provided to make clear a few points. First of all, coding is key to qualitative data analysis. If one wants to conduct qualitative research, be prepared to code. Second, coding can take various forms and shapes, but it is a systematic process that requires back and forth comparison of categories and emerging themes. Coding should not be viewed as a tidy and clear-cut process. Third, coding has two main purposes; those are thematic analysis and theory generation. Depending upon the aims of the research process, thematic analysis for purposes of theme generation only may be adequate. Otherwise, thematic analysis for purposes of theory generation may be the ultimate prize. Finally, if one wants to generate a theory, then grounded theory is the study design that should be utilized.

8

QUANTITATIVE RESEARCH DESIGNS

There are six basic designs in quantitative research: 1) experimental, 2) quasi-experimental, 3) single-subject, 4) correlational, 5) causal-comparative, and 6) survey. Each one plays the crucial role of guiding the researcher in the collection, analysis, and interpretation of data to better understand the phenomenon in which the researcher is focusing the inquiry. Quantitative research designs quantify reality (e.g., psychological test scores, seconds of attention span, frequency of off-task behaviors, range of movement angle, running speed) or code reality (e.g., married = 1, single = 2), which reflect the positivist assumption that these quantifications validly represent the phenomenon of interest. But these representations may not be comprehensive. "A major concern to researchers is that extraneous variables may explain away any results that are obtained" (Fraenkel et al., 2019, p. 334). That is, intrinsic to each quantitative research design there are a number of threats jeopardizing the study's internal validity (i.e., accuracy of results in explaining the relationships of variables) and external validity (i.e., generalization of results from the sample to the population). To the extent of what is methodologically possible, these threats must be accounted for and controlled during the formulation and implementation of any quantitative study.

Butler (2014) indicated that there are two methodologically overarching goals in quantitative research, and studies will fit one or the other:

studies that are exploratory in nature (i.e., discovery purposes, question generating) and studies that are confirmatory in nature (i.e., testing purposes, answer generating). A correlational study, for example, could be exploratory or could be confirmatory, and the same occurs with any other quantitative research design. Studies that require hypothesis testing can be quickly identified as being confirmatory (i.e., confirming whether the theoretical proposition of the hypothesis is confirmed by the findings of the study).

But, which quantitative design should the researcher choose for the study? That is one important question that becomes answered as the researcher engages in the process of carefully reviewing the literature. Given that this review will revolve around the phenomenon of interest (e.g., resilience) with the population of interest (e.g., women in juvenile detention), the literature review will help researchers detect the most appropriate research design as well as alert them of the methodological successes and errors incurred by other researchers. The literature review should also give the researcher a plethora of ideas regarding the viability of the proposed study given the researcher's own professional positionality, the time needed to successfully deploy such a study, the strategies to recruit participants, the measurements that could be used (or adapted), and the need to create new instrumentation, among other important issues. It would be a serious mistake to choose a research design without having first thoroughly reviewed the relevant literature associated with the phenomenon of interest. The remainder of this chapter will be devoted to describing the characteristics of the six aforementioned quantitative research designs as well as to present pertinent information associated with data collection and data analysis within quantitative research.

DIFFERENT QUANTITATIVE RESEARCH DESIGNS

Experimental Research

"Experimental research is one of the most powerful research methodologies that researchers can use" (Fraenkel et al., 2019, p. 259). This is the method that "provides the strongest evidence of cause-and-effect relationships" among variables (Johnson & Christensen, 2017, p. 317). Most researchers will agree that experiments require quite a number of quality technical assurances in place, requirements that are not always feasible to secure when studying human behavior (i.e., controlling situations, keeping some variables constant, standardizing procedures, eliminating the effect of confounding extraneous variables, securing various groups for comparison purposes, conducting sample randomization, conducting random assignment of participants to groups). Because of all these methodological requirements, experimental research is the only design that allows the researcher to determine, with a high degree of certainty, the cause-and-effect relationship that exists between the independent and dependent variables. This is done through the utilization of at least two groups (i.e., treatment and control). No other quantitative research design has that same degree of precision power.

According to Johnson and Christensen (2017), there are fundamentally three settings for conducting an experiment: 1) field experiments (i.e., real-life settings where not all variables can be fully controlled, but with the perk of gaining insight into naturally occurring human behaviors), 2) laboratory experiments (i.e., controlled settings where all variables can be fully controlled, but with the caveat of being an artificial environment), and 3) Internet experiments (i.e., virtual setting where various degrees of control can be exerted, but with an extraordinary capacity to overcome geographical barriers to sampling). Given these settings, Johnson and Christensen warned about the balance that researchers need to keep between the proclivity to control for potential confounding extraneous variables and the risk to lose the ability to observe naturally occurring human behavior. Johnson and Christensen have indicated that a researcher using an experimental design "sacrifices the external validity for enhanced internal validity" (p. 318). This means that in order for researchers to confirm the cause-effect relationship observed among variables, they jeopardize the study's ability to fully generalize results to the population.

At the time of the publication of this book, experimental research has been at the forefront of the global news as researchers from around the globe have conducted numerous clinical trials to demonstrate the efficiency of the COVID-19 vaccines (e.g., Pilishvili et al., 2021; Tenforde et al., 2021). These clinical trials were experiments, most of which utilized the randomized pretest-posttest control group design. There are several experimental research designs with varying degrees of strength in controlling for confounding extraneous variables (e.g., one-group pretest-posttest design, random assignment with matching, randomized Solomon four-group design). Researchers need to invest time to determine which design would best fit their inquiry. Line graphs, histograms, stem-and-leaf, boxplots, and pie charts are generally used to visually represent the impact of the independent variable on the dependent variable and to represent the characteristics of the sample participating in the study.

Figure 8.1 shows a boxplot (also known as a box-and-whiskers plot) comparing the age distribution of participants (i.e., *y* or vertical axis) by gender (i.e., *x* or horizontal axis). The graph allows the reader to quickly identify which group has a higher median age (i.e., men) and which group shows the larger age dispersion (i.e., women). In this graph, each box and its respective whiskers show how the age is spread in quartiles containing each 25% of the distribution. For example, if you look at the data collected on women, the median age is about 36 years and 50% of the group is contained in the blue box (i.e., between the ages of 30 and

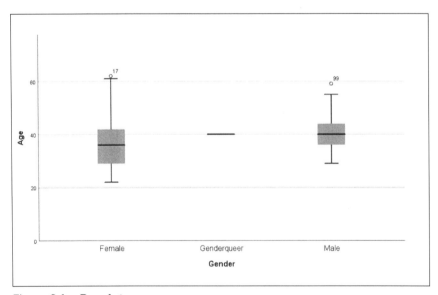

Figure 8.1. Boxplot.
Source: Suárez Sousa (2021).

42). The younger 25% has an age between 22 and 29 years, while the older 25% of the group has an age between 43 and 61 years. Boxplots are quite useful to identify any data that fall outside the upper or lower limits of the distribution. Those data pieces are known as *outliers* and represent abnormal or extreme values that, depending on the type of analysis that needs to be conducted, may need to be removed (or not) from the data set as they have the potential of skewing the results. In this specific figure, cases 17 and 99 are outliers. Notice that the number shown does not represent the data, but the specific participants (i.e., Participant 17, Participant 99) whose ages significantly differ from the ages of others.

Quasi-Experimental Research

Quasi-experimental research is quite similar to experimental research but differs in one critical component: lack of randomization for group assignment. Quasi-experimental designs may randomize for sampling purposes but cannot randomize group designation (i.e., who is assigned to the treatment group, who is assigned to the control group). There are several quasi-experimental designs (e.g., matching-only design, counterbalanced design, non-equivalent comparison-group design), and researchers would need to carefully determine which one best fits their inquiry if they desire to conduct an experiment for which randomization may not be an option (e.g., fourth-grade students receiving Title I reading services, and for whom it would be unethical to withhold said services on a random basis). Line graphs, histograms, stem-and-leaf, boxplots, and pie charts are generally used to visually represent the impact of the independent variable on the dependent variable and to represent the characteristics of the sample participating in the study.

Figure 8.2 shows a bar graph comparing the frequency of areas of expertise (i.e., y or vertical axis) by their frequency (i.e., x or horizontal axis). As it can clearly be seen, there are more participants self-identifying as experts in the Health Sciences, Language Arts, and Social Sciences teaching areas. On the other hand, participants self-identifying as experts in the Behavioral Sciences, Engineering, Physical Sciences, and Visual and Performing Arts are the least in number.

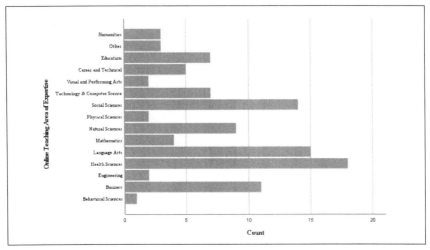

Figure 8.2. Bar Graph.
Source: McMahon (2021, p. 83).

Single-Subject Research

Single-subject research is frequently utilized in the field of special education (e.g., behavioral intervention for a child with autism) and clinical psychology (e.g., PTSD treatment for a prison inmate) in which a treatment is administered to a single person or a very small group of people that function as their own experimental and control groups (Kratochwill et al., 2010; Zettle, 2020). This design is known as the "single-case design experiment" (Barlon & Hensen, 1984, as cited by Zettle, 2020, p. 650). There are different types of single-subject designs (e.g., A-B, A-B-A-B, A-B-C-B), all of which are "adaptations of interrupted time-series design and can provide a rigorous experimental evaluation of intervention effects" (Kratochwill et al., 2010, p. 2). These designs "often involve repeated, systematic measurement of a dependent variable before, during, and after the active manipulation of an independent variable" (Kratochwill et al., 2010, p. 2). Consequently, researchers make direct attempts to carefully control and manipulate the independent variable and measure its impact on the dependent variable in a systematized way. A single-subject design uses repeated conditions of baseline (A/Baseline, i.e., natural occurrence of the dependent variable before the independent variable is implemented) and intervention (B/Treatment, i.e., the occurrence of the dependent variable during the active implementation of the independent variable). Sometimes re-searchers decide to include another intervention condition (C), which represents an intervention that differs from the previously administered (B) and also differs from the baseline (A).

The length of the study's conditions varies significantly from study to study, from conditions that last a few hours to a few weeks. What is generally agreed upon is the fact that conditions should last the same time within a given study. Given the controlled conditions that surround single-subject designs, the ability to determine cause-effect relationships between the independent and dependent variables will significantly depend on the setting where the study takes place (e.g., clinician's office versus middle school classroom). Line graphs are gen-erally used to visually represent the impact of the independent variable on the dependent variable and to represent the characteristics of the sample participating in the study.

Figure 8.3 shows a line graph of an A-B-A-C design. As you can see, this graph demonstrates how the frequency of Subject 1's response (i.e., y or vertical axis) is affected by the type of condition across a number of sessions (i.e., x or horizontal axis). During Baseline (i.e., A) the fre-quency of response does not go higher than 2 times per session. Dur-ing the implementation of the first intervention condition (i.e., B), the frequency of response increases. When the treatment is removed and

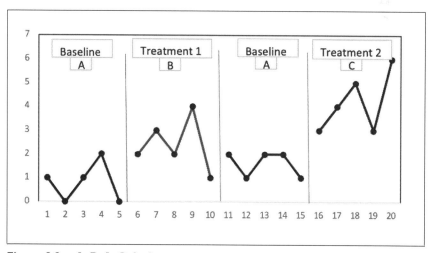

Figure 8.3.   A-B-A-C design.
Note: Adapted from Carr & Burkholder (1998).

the condition goes back to Baseline (i.e., A) the rate of frequency drops again, only to increase during the fourth and final intervention condition (i.e., C). Notice that the two intervention conditions are different (i.e., Treatment 1, Treatment 2)—thus the B and C nomenclatures.

Correlational Research

Correlational research is an umbrella term used to include designs that explore the association between two or more variables. Different from experimental, quasi-experimental, and single-subject research, correlational research does not attempt to manipulate any variables but to study them as they naturally occur. Because of that, in correlational research the terms *independent variable* and *dependent variable* are replaced by the terms *predictor* or *criterion variable*, and *outcome variable*, respectively. Additionally, correlation does not mean causation (Field, 2009; Norman & Streiner, 2008), and this is something quite important researchers need to keep in mind when selecting the correlational design that will best fit their inquiry.

All correlational designs will try to determine "the degree to which two or more quantitative variables are related, and it does so by using a correlation coefficient" (Fraenkel et al., 2019, p. 325). This correlation coefficient, which is a score that may oscillate between –1.00 and +1.00, determines the strength (i.e., value) and direction (i.e., +/–sign) of the association. "The closer it is to either of those limits, the stronger is the relationship between the two variables" (Howell, 2004). Negative correlations (i.e., indirect, high-low, low-high) describe the variables as behaving in opposite directions; that is, when the score of one variable increases, the score of the other variable decreases. For example, the more ounces of alcohol a person drinks, the less capable a person will be to walk straight for a few yards. Positive correlations (i.e., direct, high-high, low-low) describe the variables as behaving in the same direction; that is, when the score of one variable increases, the score of the other variable increases, and when the score of one variable decreases, the score of the other variable also decreases. For example, the more hours middle school students spend practicing Spanish, the higher the score on their written Spanish test. Conversely, if these students do not practice Spanish, their test scores will be quite low.

Huck (2000) stated that the central question being answered by correlational studies is "to what extent are the high scores of one variable paired with the high scores of the other variable?" (p. 61). This highlights the nature of correlational research as exploring the covariance of variables (Howell, 2004) and once again it emphasizes its lack of power in determining cause-effect relationships. Correlational research is conducted with a single group of participants and always involves the measurement of continuous (i.e., ratio) variables. Scatterplots are generally used to visually represent the correlation that exists between the predictor and outcome variables and to represent the characteristics of the sample participating in the study. Figure 8.4 shows a scatterplot graph demonstrating a positive correlation between the distribution of effective online course design practices scores (i.e., y or vertical axis) and the distribution of online teaching self-efficacy overall scores (i.e., x or horizontal axis). The positive correlation is visually clear in the upper trajectory of the dots. The researcher must remember that each participant in correlational studies has at least two scores. In this specific study, McMahon (2021) found that faculty with self-appraised high online teaching self-efficacy also identified themselves as highly effective in the practices of designing online instruction (and vice versa).

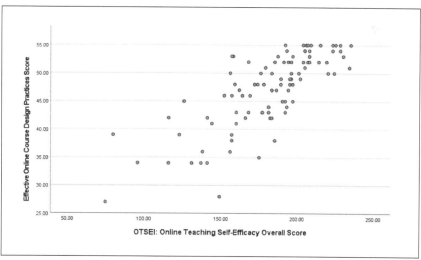

Figure 8.4. Scatterplot.
Source: McMahon (2021, p. 93).

Causal-Comparative Research

Causal-comparative research, like correlational research, does not attempt to manipulate any variables but to study them as they naturally occur. Similarly, the focus of causal-comparative studies is to explore "the cause or consequences of differences that already exist between or among groups of individuals" (Fraenkel et al., 2019, p. 344). This type of research, like correlational studies, is also considered associational research (Fraenkel et al., 2019). An important difference with correlational research is that causal-comparative studies measure the effect of a criterion or predictor variable on an outcome variable that has been linked in the past and whose association can be studied in the present time. This is why this type of study is "also referred to sometimes as *ex post facto* (from the Latin for 'after the fact') *research*" (Fraenkel et al., 2019, p. 344). For example, if a researcher is interested in exploring the role that having a Hispanic elementary teacher plays in the academic achievement of Hispanic students in her class, then the study's criterion or predictor variable would be the race of the teacher while the outcome variable would be the Hispanic students' academic performance.

In order to determine the role played by having a Hispanic teacher in Hispanic students' academic performance, the researcher should recruit another elementary teacher (preferably with an elementary degree and similar teaching experience) from a different race whose classroom demographics include Hispanic students (preferably in the same proportion as the classroom of the Hispanic teacher). In this manner, the researcher can compare the role that having a Hispanic teacher plays on Hispanic students' academic performance, that is, students who have been exposed to her teaching for a number of months prior to the beginning of the study.

Although data are collected in the present time, causal-comparative research has a retrospective component regarding the association that has existed between the variables being studied. Causal-comparative research is conducted with two or more groups of participants, and "typically involve at least one categorical variable (group membership)" (Fraenkel et al., 2019, p. 346). Histograms, stem-and-leaf, boxplots, and pie charts are generally used to visually represent the association that exists between the predictor and outcome variables and to represent the characteristics of the sample participating in the study.

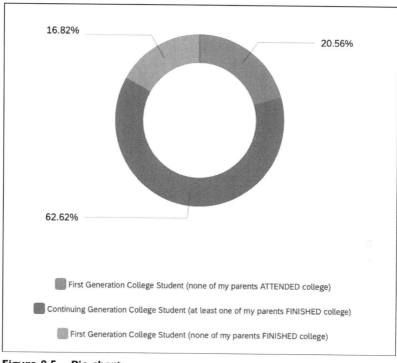

Figure 8.5.   Pie chart.
Source: Suárez Sousa (2021).

Figure 8.5 shows a pie chart depicting the distribution of a group of students regarding their college first-generation status. The pie chart clearly demonstrates that the largest subgroup is composed of continuing generation college students (i.e., defined as a student with at least one parent finishing college), which make up 62.62% of the sample of this study.

Survey Research

Survey research has the main focus of collecting data on specific issues (e.g., opinions about COVID-19 vaccines, stress associated to COVID-19) with the purpose of describing the profile of the population who have experienced those issues according to demographic variables of interest (e.g., race, age, level of education, occupation). Researchers using survey research must design a questionnaire, which is the primary data collection tool in this type of research. Survey research could be conducted in-person (i.e., interview), virtually (e.g., interview mediated by a virtual platform), long distance with no contact (e.g., electronic questionnaire sent via email), or by phone. The questionnaire could be administered by the researcher (e.g., interview) or be self-administered by the participant (e.g., returnable electronic questionnaire via email).

Two important options the researcher needs to consider when conducting survey research relate to the phenomenon being studied. Option one, if the questionnaire will collect data on participants' opinions, then the questions can be freely formulated and do not need to undergo any technical process other than the researcher feeling confident regarding the instrument's questions being aligned to the study's research questions. The researcher will also need to pay attention to a few other things, namely: whether there is a good combination of questions (e.g., multiple choice), whether the instrument has an adequate number of questions (e.g., avoid saturation), whether the instrument has a clear navigable answering system (e.g., Likert scale), and whether the wording is also clear (e.g., avoid double-barreled questions). The researcher also needs to take the time to investigate best practices in the construction of a robust questionnaire before it is distributed.

Option two, if the questionnaire will collect data on any type of psychoeducational (e.g., chemistry proficiency) or psychological (e.g., stress) construct with the purpose of determining how much of this construct participants possess or are experiencing at a given time, then the questionnaire needs to undergo a more involved process during its development. This process aims to secure three fundamental things: 1) that the questions being asked are aligned to the theoretical structure of the construct being measured, 2) that the questionnaire is evaluated by a panel of subject matter experts (SMEs) with the task of determining the instrument's coefficient of content validity (see Lawshe, 1975), and 3) that the questionnaire is piloted with the purpose of determining the instrument's coefficient of reliability. Validity and reliability are essential in the process of securing the instrument's technical quality assurance.

If option two is the route the researcher needs to take, then the researcher needs first to identify the theoretical framework that defines the construct of interest in a manner that is in agreement to the researcher's professional stance or philosophy. This theory will provide guidelines regarding the construct's theoretical components that should be reflected in the questions asked in the questionnaire. While this is a complex process, it is quite feasible to accomplish as part of a research project provided that time is not an issue. Histograms and pie charts are generally used to visually represent data from survey research focused on participants' opinions. Scatterplots, box plots, histograms, and pie charts are generally used to visually represent data from survey research measuring psychoeducational or psychological constructs and to represent the characteristics of the sample participating in the study.

Survey Research Return Rate

When conducting survey research, it is quite critical that the researcher calculates and reports the survey's return rate, and that the elements included in table 8.1 are used in order to achieve that goal adequately. Knowing the return rate provides the researcher with context to better understand the obtained results. For example, some topics are of more interest than others or are more sensitive to others. The researcher can appraise those levels of impact by knowing who were tried to recruit and who ended up self-selecting to participate in the study. While the researcher can use randomization to select the sample, survey research, generally speaking, uses convenience or purposeful sampling.

Table 8.1.   Calculation of Return Rate.

Elements of the Formula		Example
Primary Rejection: The invitation to participate was not returned (R1)	Count the frequency of cases	12563
Secondary Rejection: Incomplete survey (R2)	Count the frequency of cases	54
Total of participants who responded to the survey (N)	Count the frequency of cases	1367
Response Rate	N/(R1+R2+N)*100	9.78%
	This is reported as a percentage	

Source: Instituto de Estudios Peruanos (2021, p. 5).

THREATS TO THE INTERNAL AND EXTERNAL VALIDITY OF THE DESIGN

The preceding section described the six existing quantitative research designs. It is important that the researcher is aware that each one of these is vulnerable to threats that jeopardize the study's internal and external validity. Internal validity refers to the power that the study has to confirm that the obtained results are accurate and that the cause-effect or the associative relationships between variables in the study do exist in reality. External validity refers to the power that the study has to generalize the results to the population from which the sample was extracted. It is the researcher's responsibility to learn what these threats are, how to control them to the greatest extent, and how to methodologically account for them in the design of the study.

Table 8.2 presents the most commonly described threats to the internal validity of quantitative research designs. The primary threat to the external validity of a quantitative study results from the sampling strategy used; that is why there is no section in the table associated to the external validity. True random sampling procedures are the ones highly associated with the strength of the external validity of a given study and are recommended the most to address this threat.

Table 8.2. Threats to the Internal Validity of Quantitative Research Designs.

Research Design	Threats to the Internal Validity of the Design
Experimental	Subject characteristics, mortality, location, instrument decay, data collector characteristics, data collector bias, testing, history, maturation, attitude of subjects, regression, implementation (p. 274).
Single-Subject	Length of baseline condition, length of intervention conditions, number of variables changed when moving from one condition to another, degree and speed of any change that occurs, a return— or not—of the behavior to baseline levels, independence of behaviors, number of baselines (p. 302).
	Location, data collector characteristics, maturation, regression, instrument decay, data collector bias, attitudinal, and implementation threads (p. 307).
Correlational	Alternative explanations for relationships found in the data (p. 334).
	Subject characteristics, location, instrumentation decay, data collector characteristics, data collector bias, testing, mortality (pp. 335–338).
Causal-Comparative	Subject characteristics, mortality, location, instrument decay, data collector characteristics, data collector bias, implementation, history, maturation, regression (pp. 350–351).
Survey	Mortality, location, instrumentation, instrument decay (p. 374).

Source: Fraenkel et al. (2019).

TIME IN QUANTITATIVE RESEARCH

Time is an important criterion when designing a quantitative study. The methodology chosen to align with the research questions will dictate the amount of time needed to conduct the study. Some studies are quite short, while others take a significant amount of time to complete. There are three different types of studies that differ by virtue of the time required in their methodology (i.e., cross-sectional, longitudinal, retrospective).

Cross-Sectional Research

Cross-sectional research is data "collected from the research participants at a single point in time or during a single, relatively brief time period" (Johnson & Christensen, 2017, p. 401). This does not mean that the data are all collected on a single day or even on a single week, but rather that the data collection period takes place in the span of a few days or even a few weeks. This type of data collection is vulnerable to the events surrounding the lives of participants at the time of contact.

Longitudinal Research

Longitudinal research is data "collected at more than one time point or during more than one data-collection period, and the researcher is interested in making comparisons across time" (Johnson & Christensen, 2017, p. 402). This type of study may take from a few months to several years to be completed. In quantitative research, longitudinal studies are quite common when researchers address issues related to human development (e.g., early childhood, aging, cultural adaptation, second language acquisition).

Retrospective Research

When conducting retrospective research, the researcher "moves backward in time" to collect individuals' data that "help explain individuals' current status" (Johnson & Christensen, 2017, p. 405). This is achieved either by virtue of participants' recollections from memory of past events or by accessing participants' personal records (e.g., medical, academic). In some studies, no individuals are required to directly participate (e.g., college graduation trends of minority students for the past 10 years) as all the relevant required data can be retrieved from archives.

QUANTITATIVE DATA ANALYSIS

Sampling

Researchers, generally speaking, cannot recruit an entire population for a given study simply because of logistical complexities, time, and financial constraints, which is why recruiting a representative random sample is the most viable option. The idea is that the random sample will generate information that can be validly inferred to the population from where it was drawn. However, this inferencing process has an embedded procedural error called *Standard Error of the Sample* (also called *Standard Error of the Sample Mean*). If the researcher considers that all populations are large (e.g., students from all Minnesota state colleges and universities) and also considers the composition of all possible random samples that could be recruited, the researcher can deduce that not all of these samples would be quite the same, and consequently, the data obtained from each one of them would not be the exact same, either, every time a sample is drawn. Even though all of these random samples would be coming from the exact same population, the data are going to unequivocally vary. That variability across all possible random samples is called Standard Error of the Sample, and while there is no way to control it, there is a way to account for it when reporting the results from a study. It is important to remember that "the standard error falls as the sample size increases, as the extent of chance variation is reduced" (Altman & Bland, 2005). Consequently, the recommendation to reduce this error is to aim for a large random sample size whenever possible.

Ideally, the researcher would recruit a random sample for the study; that essentially means each participant has the exact same chance to be recruited for the study; however, this is not always possible. As a matter of fact, depending on the researcher's area of practice, this option would be more elusive than not. What is quite important is that the researcher has a clear understanding of who constitutes the population from which to draw the sample, what the study's research questions are, what the study's research design is, and then make a decision about which sampling strategy (e.g., random, non-random, cluster, convenience, purposive) would be the best fit for the study given all the aforementioned elements.

There are two very important concepts that need to be differentiated because they carry the same meaning but are applied to different groups: 1) *statistic* is an observation obtained with the sample of a given study, and 2) *parameter* is the calculated observation in the population. Each statistic plays a proxy role to the population's parameter. The study will produce many different statistics with the goal of knowing their respective parameters. This is the generalizability of a study, that is, how much the results from the sample can be generalized to the population. The degree of generalizability is strictly determined by the sample of a study. From this, it is reiterated that the sampling process is quite an important element in any study's methodology.

Sample Size

How many participants in a sample are sufficient? Well, there are some important questions to ask first before the researcher answers that question. For example, will the study explore the phenomenon as occurring within a single group? Will the study explore the phenomenon as occurring in three different groups or the same group at three different times? As it may be correctly assumed, different research designs have different needs for data collection and data analysis purposes. If the study requires a single group, maybe 30 participants would be sufficient, but if the study requires three different groups, then 90 participants would become the sampling goal. Again, the research questions provide a clear path to the determination of the study's sample size as well as the sampling strategy. Table 8.3 shows the different formulas available for the calculation of sample sizes, and table 8.4 will guide the researcher through the process of executing the formula that is needed based on the study's research design. Currently, there are programs available on the Internet that help researchers calculate the sample size needed for

Table 8.3.   Formulas to Calculate Sample Size.

Variables	One Group	Two Groups (n = per group)
Nominal, ordinal, or interval variables	To estimate a proportion: $n = Z\alpha^2 * p * q / d^2$ (Unknown population size) To estimate a proportion: $n = N* Z\alpha^2 * p * q /$ $d^2*(N-1)+ Z\alpha^2 * p * q$ (Known population size)	To compare two proportions: $n = [Z\alpha*\sqrt{2p(1-p)}+ Z\beta*\sqrt{P_1(1-p_1)}+P_2(1-p_2)]^2/$ $(P_1-P_2)^2$
Ratio variables	To estimate a mean: $n = Z\alpha^2 * S^2/d^2$ (Unknown population size) To estimate a mean: $n = N* Z\alpha^2 * S^2/$ $d^2*(N-1)+ Z\alpha^2 * S^2$ (Known population size)	To compare two means: $n = 2 (Z\alpha+ Z\beta)^2*S^2/d^2$

Source: Navarro (2020).

a given study. If the researcher has access to Microsoft Excel or the Statistical Packet for the Social Sciences (or any other statistical software), sample size can also be calculated by using those programs. While directions on how to execute these calculations can be found on the Internet, the researcher must ensure the source is reliable.

If a random sample cannot be obtained, the researcher may consider doubling the recommended sample size and opting for a convenience sampling process instead. The researcher should keep in mind that a convenience sampling process could be stratified or clustered to respond to the needs of the study (e.g., the researcher needs students from specific schools within a school district). The researcher must make sure to report in detail the strategy used to draw the sample from the population of study. See textbox 8.1 (Carlson, 2020, p. 37) for a narrative presented to describe sampling procedures.

Table 8.4. Important Elements to Consider When Calculating Sample Size.

Type of Variables	Number of Groups	Purpose	Size of the Population	Confidence[1]	Significance[2] (α) (α = Type I Error/ Reject H0 when is true)	Power[3] (1-β) (β = Type II Error/ Accept H0 when is false)
Nominal, Ordinal, or Interval	1 group	Estimate a proportion (%)		95%	For a confidence of 95%: $\alpha = .05$ (Directional Hypothesis: $Z\alpha = 1.645$) (Non-Directional Hypothesis: $Z\alpha = 1.960$)	1-β = 80% ($\beta = .20$) ($Z\beta = 0.842$)
	2 or more groups	Compare two or more proportions	Known			
Ratio (i.e., continuous)	1 group	Estimate a mean	or	99%	For a confidence of 99%: $\alpha = .01$ (Directional Hypothesis: $Z\alpha = 2.326$) (Non-Directional Hypothesis: $Z\alpha = 2.576$)	1-β = 90% ($\beta = .10$) ($Z\beta = 1.282$)
	2 or more groups	Compare two or more means	Unknown			

TEXTBOX 8.1.
Sampling Procedure

Sampling. Participants for the study were selected based on a nonrandom, convenience sampling. Program officials require all teacher preparation candidates to complete the edTPA performance assessment during their student teaching semester, which makes all students eligible for inclusion, yet the completion rate is around 88%. During student teaching, teacher candidates are provided time to complete the CM Exit Survey during their professional development conference held on campus, so completion rates are typically high as well. However, after the first year of teaching concludes these candidates are asked to respond to the CM Transition to Teaching Survey. Because one year has passed since being enrolled in university, not all students, now alumni, choose to participate. All students who graduated between 2015–2018 who have the four variables: a completed edTPA; CM Exit Survey; CM Transition to Teaching Survey; and CM Supervisor Survey on file with the institution, were utilized for the quantitative portion of this study. The response rate of the surveys is indicated in Table 3.

Descriptive Statistics

After the data collection phase has concluded, the data analysis process begins. This process can be quite long, depending on the type and number of research questions that need to be addressed. Descriptive statistics have the purpose of summarizing the study's results and to "describe the basic features of the data sets" (Hassani et al., 2010, p. 108). This task is completed by displaying the data in an organized manner through the utilization of tables, figures, or both and by presenting the data in compact indices (Huck, 2000). There are two basic types of compact indices or descriptive statistics: 1) measures of central tendency (i.e., median, mean, mode), which are "numerical values that refer to the center of the distribution" (Howell, 2004, p. 60, and 2) measures of dispersion or variability (i.e., standard deviation, range, variance), representing "the degree to which individual data points are distributed around the mean" (Howell, 2004, p. 73). Manikandan (2011) warned that "the measures of central tendency are not adequate to describe data" and that "two data sets can have the same mean but they can be entirely different" from each other (p. 315). For this reason, the researcher must always report measures of dispersion along measures of central tendency and use both to gain insight into the data sets.

Several authors suggest starting the summary process by graphing the data through one or more of the following options (e.g., Howell, 2004): 1) simple, grouped (i.e., by intervals), and cumulative frequency distributions; 2) stem-and-leaf displays; 3) histograms; 4) bar graphs; 5) frequency polygons; and 6) pie graphs (Huck, 2000; Norman & Streiner, 2008). Simple, grouped, and cumulative frequency distribution tables will help the researcher "better understand the characteristics of the subjects involved in a study" (Huck, 2000, p. 21), providing a good summary profile. Stem-and-leaf tables display the distribution of the universe of scores from a given variable, providing the researcher with a comprehensive and detailed view of every single score.

Different from frequency distribution tables, histograms are graphical displays of frequency distributions for numeric data. Histograms are always formatted in the same way, that is, the horizontal axis (x) represents the interval scores (e.g., 11–20, 21–30) from lower to higher (or "numerically logical," Huck, 2000, p. 26) on contiguous boxes, while the vertical axis (y) represents the frequencies. Bar graphs are like histograms, only that these are used for the display of categorical data (e.g., married, single), and because of that, there is no specific order in which categories are presented on the horizontal axis.

Next, frequency polygons (a.k.a., line graphs) are quite similar to histograms in that these display numeric data, only that the vertical axis may include frequencies or percentages. The difference from histograms is that "each bar is replaced with a single dot positioned where the top of the bar would have been located, then adjacent dots are connected with straight lines to form the final graph" (Huck, 2000, p. 27). If the researcher wants to display the shape of the distribution, or have a sense of the overall "area" of the distribution, it would be best to use the frequency polygons, which can also display cumulative frequency distributions and are helpful when analyzing a variable over time (e.g., increase of COVID-19 cases in the last year). Finally, pie graphs are an "easy-to-understand way of showing how a full group is made up of subgroups, and also of showing the relative size of the subgroups" (Huck,

2000, p. 28). The only recommendation is to use pie graphs when there are no more than six to eight sub-groups; otherwise the pie becomes sliced into too many pieces and becomes hard to understand.

Group designs, such as experimental, quasi-experimental, and causal-comparative, focus on the comparison of the dependent variables across groups, or a comparison of pre- and post-treatment phases. Because of that, groups' means and standard deviations will need to be calculated for comparison purposes. If the study is confirmatory in nature, inferential statistics would be required in order to determine, for example, whether the mean values of different groups are indeed different. Also, in confirmatory studies, the initial visual inspection of the data is instrumental to appraise the degree of normality of the distribution of the dependent or outcome variable. Normality is one of several statistical assumptions required for decision-making regarding the use of parametric inferential tests versus non-parametric inferential tests for hypothesis testing purposes.

Inferential Statistics

Inferential statistics are used to "draw conclusions that extend beyond the specific data that are collected" because the "data are considered to represent a sample—and the goal of the investigation is to make one or more statements about the larger group of which the sample is only a part" (Huck, 2000, p. 111). Specifically, when the researcher is interested in testing the study's null hypothesis and make a determination about whether to reject it or not, inferential statistics must be used. As Huck (2000) stated, "the term inferential statistics is used to label the portion of statistics dealing with the principles and techniques that allow researchers to generalize their findings beyond the actual data sets obtained" (p. 111), that is, from the sample of the study to the population. Inferential procedures are conducted because it would be quite difficult to expose, for example, each elementary-age student to a summer literacy academy with the purpose of determining how much it buffers the detrimental effect of the summer slide on students' reading performance. Rather, it is quite optimal to select a sample from the population of elementary-age students and test the impact of the literacy academy on just them.

Table 8.5. Commonly Used Inferential Statistics by Quantitative Research Design.

Research Design	Parametric Test Assumptions-dependent	Non-Parametric Test Assumptions-freer[1]
Experimental, Quasi-Experimental, Single-Subject, Causal-Comparative, Survey	• Independent Samples t-Test • Dependent Samples t-Test • One-Way ANOVA • Repeated Measures ANOVA • MANOVA • Factor Analysis	• Mann-Whitney U/ Independent Groups • Wilcoxon's Matched-Pairs Signed-Ranked Test/ Dependent Groups • Kruskal-Wallis ANOVA/ Independent Groups • Friedman's ANOVA/ Dependent Groups • Multivariate Kruskal-Wallis • (MKW) • Chi-Square Test of Independence (CAT)
Correlational, Survey	Pearson Product Moment Correlation Hierarchical Regression	Spearman Correlation
	Multiple Regression	Kernel Regression

Source: Sheskin (2000), Field (2009), Huck (2000), Howell (2004), Norman & Streiner (2008).

There are several inferential statistics utilized with the various quantitative research designs, that is, when these are confirmatory in nature. Table 8.5 presents a list of inferential statistics aligned to research designs. The table lists parametric tests as well as non-parametric tests. The researcher must be aware that this is not a comprehensive table by any means. It is the researcher's responsibility to determine the best inferential statistical fit for the study based on the study's design (e.g., survey, causal-comparative), number of groups involved, their relationship (e.g., related samples, independent samples), and the scale of measurement used to collect data regarding the variables of the study (e.g., categorical, continuous).

Statistical Assumptions

In order to use parametric tests, first the researcher needs to check whether the data's statistical assumptions required have been met. If statistical assumptions are violated, then "we stop being able to draw accurate conclusions about reality" (Field, 2009, p. 132). As Field (2009) so compellingly stated, "different statistical models assume different things, and if these models are going to reflect reality accurately then these assumptions need to be true" (p. 132). An important step is to determine which statistical test best fits the study's hypothesis, then determine the test's statistical assumptions. For example, many researchers use parametric statistical tests like the Pearson Product Moment Correlation, which require the confirmation of the normality assumption (i.e., scores are normally distributed). If this assumption is violated, then the researcher will have to use the equivalent non-parametric statistical test, which in this case would be the Spearman Correlation. The researcher can quickly visualize the normality assumption by generating a frequency polygon, for example, in order to check whether the normality assumption has been violated or not. However, the visual inspection can be limiting and the researcher will still need to check whether the distribution has or has not met the cutoff skewness and kurtosis values.

Each inferential parametric statistical test (e.g., t-Test) has its own set of assumptions (e.g., normality, homogeneity of variance), each assumption needs to be tested (e.g., Shapiro-Wilk or Kolmogorov-Smirnov Tests for normality, Levene Test for homogeneity of variance), and confirmation must be provided to indicate whether all the assumptions have been satisfied (i.e., use the parametric test) or have been violated (i.e., use the non-parametric equivalent). Most statistical software programs (e.g., SPSS, Excel) can support the researcher with this assumption testing process in a very efficient manner. It is the researcher's responsibility to explore, in a great level of detail, the assumptions that need to be checked, and that these are reported for dissertation, conference, or manuscript writing purposes.

Effect Size

The effect size of a confirmatory quantitative study's results refers to the "measure of the magnitude of an observed effect" (Field, 2009, p. 785). Each quantitative design will require a specific effect size calculation, but the most commonly reported ones are Cohen's d, Glass's g, and Pearson's r (Field, 2009). It is the researcher's responsibility to explore, in a great level of detail, the effect size that needs to be reported based on the inferential statistic used in the study.

Confidence Intervals

The confidence intervals account for the standard error associated with the estimation of the parameter. The confidence interval is reported with the purpose of accounting for the embedded procedural error (i.e., Standard Error of the Sample, described earlier in this chapter), and to provide an accurate range of the statistic obtained to better formulate the value of the parameter. For example, the mean academic growth obtained by a group of fifth-grade students on a standardized math test after five months of implementing the cover-copy-compare (CCC) instructional strategy is 15 points with a confidence interval of 3 points. Then, the interpretation is that the academic growth of any group of fifth-grade students (taken randomly from the sample) who were exposed to the same instructional strategy for five months, would oscillate between 12 and 18 points. The confidence intervals (CI) must always be reported in the results of the study. These can be calculated based on the Standard Error of the Sample, which has the following formula: SES = SD/√(Sample Size) (Altman & Bland, 2005). Altman and Bland (2005) recommend that a 95% confidence interval can be calculated by multiplying 1.96 times the Standard Error of the Sample and adding and subtracting this resulting amount to the obtained mean. Using our previous example, the researcher would report the mean growth as well as the CI as follows: There is a 95% likelihood that the observed growth will oscillate between 12 and 18 growth points (15 ± 3).

Hypothesis Testing

Hypothesis testing is one important step required in data analysis and interpretation within confirmatory research. This testing allows the researcher to validly infer conclusions observed in the study's sample to the population the sample represents. Consequently, this is quite an important step in the study and needs to be carefully completed. Huck (2000, p. 211) recommended the following steps to conduct hypothesis testing:

1. State the null hypothesis, H_0
2. State the alternative hypothesis, H_a
3. Specify the desired level of significance, α
4. Specify the desired level of power, $1-\beta$
5. Determine the proper size of the sample(s)
6. Collect and analyze the sample data
7. Refer to a criterion for assessing the sample evidence
8. Make a decision to discard/retain H_0

These steps should provide the quality assurance to validly test the null hypothesis so that the researcher can either accept it or reject it. If the latter occurs, the researcher proceeds to accept the alternative hypothesis. Having a solid understanding of the following will serve the researcher well when testing the study's hypothesis: 1) research design, 2) threats to the study's internal and external validity, 3) variables being studied, 4) instrumentation, 5) the descriptive statistics used, and 6) the inferential statistic selected to test the hypothesis. The researcher must remember that the null hypothesis always states that there is no difference (no effect, no association) between the variables studied. Whatever results obtained from the study should be inferred to also be occurring in the population the sample was extracted from. The process of hypothesis testing can encounter errors. The most common hypothesis testing errors are Type I Error and Type II Error. The researcher needs to remain vigilant when designing, conducting, and analyzing data from the study to avoid committing either one of these.

Type I Error (α): Finding a Difference That Is Not There. The researcher believes that the Null Hypothesis (H_0) is false when in reality it is true and consequently the H_0 is rejected. Alpha represents Type I Error. Type I Errors are accounted for by determining the level of significance at .05 or lower. In theory, the lower the level of significance for hypothesis testing purposes (i.e., .05 or lower), the lower the chances of incurring in Type I Error.

Type II Error (β): Not Finding a Difference That Is There. The researcher believes that the Null Hypothesis (H_0) is true when in reality it is false and consequently the H_0 is accepted. Beta represents Type II Error and $1-\beta$ represents the power of the study. Type II Errors are accounted for by determining the level of power at .80 or higher. In theory, the higher the power of the study for hypothesis testing purposes (i.e., larger sample size), the lower the chances of incurring in Type II Error.

APA Notation

Once the researcher has concluded the data analysis, the researcher needs to proceed to report the study's findings. There is a standardized notation style used to report statistical results, and a sample of this type of notation was presented earlier in Chapter 5 (i.e., Table 5.11). The standardized notation requirements slightly vary depending on the inferential statistic being reported, and these should be used only when reporting statistically significant findings. When the finding is not statistically significant, the researcher can say so within a regular text narrative. In general, it is important to remember the following: 1) all statistical symbols must be written in italics (e.g., n, SD, p, r); 2) use two decimal points when reporting measures of central tendency, dispersion, and the values resulting from the inferential tests; 3) report levels of significance; 4) report effect size of the findings; and 5) report the confidence intervals at 95%.

CONCLUSION

This chapter is quite comprehensive in nature as it provides a focused description of the various quantitative research designs, the various strategies used for data analysis, and data visual representation. While this chapter served as a general platform for savoring what each design can provide to the study, researchers need to further explore the methodological details that will be instrumental in conducting their inquiry successfully. It is quite important that the researchers consider what their professional positionality is and because of that, consider the specific resources they have at their disposal for the successful execution of the study (e.g., time, contacts, setting, prospective participants, funds) and for its overall viability.

9

GENERAL RESEARCH ITEMS

MISCELLANEOUS PAGES

In research, there are some general items that are easiest to describe as miscellaneous pages. These pages are situated prior to the research manuscript proper, and they are sometimes optional. These pages include: a copyright page; a signature page; a dedication; and acknowledgments.

Copyright Page

A copyright page is included for theses, dissertations, and books, but they tend to be optional for other manuscript submissions. The best advice is to consult with one's adviser, publisher, or journal contact to verify whether a copyright page would be necessary. For theses and dissertations, programs often provide thesis or dissertation templates that would note whether a copyright page should be included.

Signature Page

A signature page is standard for many theses and dissertations. As with the copyright page, one should check with a program adviser to determine the placement of the signature page and other relevant information regarding it. Master's and doctoral degree programs often include templates that would make clear the expectations of a signature page.

Dedication

Larger works, such as theses, dissertations, and books, often include a dedication page. This page is optional, however. If one chooses to include a dedication page, the individual(s) to whom the work is dedicated is someone of special importance to the author.

Acknowledgments

The acknowledgments page is a standard inclusion in larger works. As a general rule, the author would acknowledge those who have played a part in supporting the author's efforts as a scholar. These individuals often include faculty members, colleagues, family members, and friends.

Abstract

An abstract is required for all research submissions, whether a journal article manuscript, thesis, or dissertation. Books tend to utilize prefaces in lieu of abstracts, but other forms of scholarship utilize abstracts. Abstracts provide a brief overview of one's research, and they are designed to give the potential reader an idea as to whether the research project would be of interest and relevance. According to USC Libraries (2021, para. 1),

> An abstract summarizes, usually in one paragraph of 300 words or less, the major aspects of the entire paper in a prescribed sequence that includes: 1) the overall purpose of the study and the research problem(s) you investigated; 2) the basic design of the study; 3) major findings or trends found as a result of your analysis; and, 4) a brief summary of your interpretations and conclusions.

An abstract should avoid citations, and it should capture the essence of the study, its findings, and the interpretation of the findings. In her abstract, Kristjansson-Nelson (2020a) exemplified the aforementioned four basic parts of an abstract by providing the purpose, the design study, findings, and the summary of the results (see textbox 9.1).

TEXTBOX 9.1.
Abstract

ABSTRACT

Inclusive media arts education should be accessible for all young people so that they can be successful citizens of this media-rich, media-saturated world. Issues surrounding access and exclusion are complex. What barriers contribute to exclusion within media arts education programs? The purpose of this study is to determine how best to create more inclusion in media arts education through leadership practices. More specifically, how do we become more inclusive in filmmaking practice, and what is the role of leadership in that endeavor? This study strives to determine how leadership best serves a highly successful inclusive media arts organization, and to make recommendations based on the findings with the aim of transferability to other media arts education programs. Through the paradigm of pragmatism, grounded theory qualitative research occurred at Bus Stop Films, an accessible film studies program that makes inclusive films located in Sydney, Australia. Interviews, a focus group, and observations were used during data collection. Research participants included administrators, teachers, staff, and students. Themes were drawn from the data using open, selective, and axial coding. Participants defined what *success* means to them, which traits and qualities are necessary to *leadership* in that environment, and what *inclusive* media arts means to them. The primary research question is as follows: How does leadership impact the success of inclusive media arts programs? Four major themes emerged from the data: *inclusive leadership, dimensions of filmmaking culture, inclusive filmmaking practice,* and *purpose.* The findings of this study led to the development of *The Theory of Dispositions in Filmmaking,* which posits that disposition serves as an active catalyst within leadership practices and filmmaking practices in media arts education programs.

LIST OF REFERENCES

In the process of writing the dissertation, conference presentation, manuscript, or technical report, the author referenced quite a number of scholarly works published by a myriad of authors. These individuals' books, articles, technical reports, websites, and more played a crucial supporting role in the entire process. It has been assumed that the list of references provides evidence of the author's "ability to engage in an extensive scholarly endeavor" (Buttlar, 1999, as cited in Tuñón & Brydges, 2006, p. 460) and that this was "characterized by locating, evaluating, synthesizing information in specific areas of study" (Tuñón & Brydges, 2006, p. 460). The list of references should reflect an honest effort and commitment made by the author to be as exhaustive and as careful as possible to gain a comprehensive understanding of the phenomenon that is the focus of the author's inquiry.

While writing the list of references could be a relatively simple mechanical process, Pemberton (2012) recommended that "creating the reference list as citations are used is a helpful strategy, because it is difficult and time-consuming to go back later and track down source citation information" (p. 86). Nowadays, some authors will make use of formatting software (e.g., http://perrla.com) available to automatically create the list of references. The author needs to choose the option that best fits their preference. Lastly, the list of references must follow a prescribed formatting that responds to the requirements of the author's discipline or professional affiliation. For example, the psychology and education professional fields use the formatting recommended by the American Psychological Association (APA)'s *Publication Manual* (7th ed.). Finally, authors should remember that all entries in the list of references should have been referred to in the body of the work.

APPENDIX

The appendix is "supplementary material usually attached at the end of a piece of writing" (Merriam-Webster, 2021). As such, the author has plenty of discretionary decision-making regarding what to include there; authors should think of it as a repository of sorts. Common entries, for example, include the IRB authorization form, copies of the instruments used for data collection (e.g., questionnaires, checklists), and tables containing raw data that the author may deem important to share with the readers. Authors must remember that in some situations they will have no room for an appendix (e.g., manuscript), but when an appendix can be included, the appendix entries "should appear and be lettered in the order they are referred to in the document" (Pemberton, 2012, p. 86). Authors must always make sure that the appendix entries are well formatted and are of quality resolution so that they could be reproduced.

CURRICULUM VITAE

The curriculum vitae commonly used in academia is a document that starts with the author's name and contact information (i.e., email, phone number) followed by these components: 1) education (i.e., degrees, years, and institutions), 2) professional experience (i.e., practitioner's experience), 3) academic experience (i.e., teaching), 4) scholarly work (e.g., grants, publications, presentations, awards), 5) service (e.g., institution, community, professional organizations), 6) professional memberships, 7) any other skills (e.g., certifications), and 8) names of professional references (only if this CV will be submitted as part of a job searching process). Authors should try to be succinct in their wording, but comprehensive in showcasing all that they have done professionally. Authors should not be shy or feel the need to be humble when writing their CV. One important consideration when writing a CV for job application purposes, however, is to ensure that the vacancy notice requirements are particularly highlighted within the CV.

TIPS AND RESOURCES

A few tips stand out based on our work with doctoral students writing their dissertation proposals and final products as well as our own scholarly projects: 1) make the scholarly work a priority, investing at least a few hours each week; 2) remain open to receive constructive feedback about the work that has been written (i.e., it is not about the author, it is about what the author has produced at a given time); 3) focus on developing cognitive stamina (i.e., sustained cognitive engagement with academic work for long periods of time); and 4) when the author gets frustrated, remember that academic work is a highly privileged activity.

When it comes to the specific style of writing, one important recommendation is to avoid an excessive use of the passive voice. The passive voice is formed by the following grammatical formula: "Passive Subject + To Be + Past Participle" (Moaddab, 2014, p. 1413), which to some may sound too impersonal (e.g., the constructive feedback was well taken by me). Contrary to passive voice, active voice seems to be more direct, clearer, and also more persuasive (e.g., I took well the constructive feedback). The following examples compare the passive and active voice:

- The researcher obtained permission from participants. (Active)
- Information was obtained from participants. (Passive)
- The researcher utilized a grounded theory approach. (Active)
- A grounded theory approach was utilized by the researcher. (Passive)
- The participants completed questionnaires. (Active)
- Questionnaires were completed by participants. (Passive)

Fortunately for authors, the software used should alert them that the passive voice is being used via a colorful line under the typed words.

Finally, a big resource for those new to conducting statistical analysis is Laerd Statistics (laerd.com). This is a website that requires a very low-cost yearly subscription and that walks the reader through theoretical context and step-by-step guidelines to run the statistical analysis while also providing accurate interpretations of the results. This site was discovered by one doctoral student and has been recommended to many ever since.

APA Requirements

Both authors are professors of education and in their scholarly work, as well as the work of their students, they use the *Publication Manual of the American Psychological Association* (APA, 2020). This manual, now in its seventh edition, provides detailed description about what scholarly writing should look like, how to format the work, how to use in-text citations as well as to create the list of references, and how to present tables and figures, among other important things. The authors strongly recommend the researcher to purchase the APA *Publication Manual* and to keep a copy nearby the researcher's writing area.

CONCLUSION

Researcher Coach was written with a sole purpose in mind: to give researchers sufficient theoretical and practical support so that they gain a sense of self-direction and autonomy in the process of formulating and conducting their research. Granted, researchers will encounter a myriad of other crucial variables (e.g., funding, time management, scheduling, prompt communications, data management) that need to be accounted for in order to increase the viability of their research. However, those variables, the authors believe, are part of the regular exercise of any professional's executive functioning skills. *Researcher Coach* focuses on the components that will account for the robustness and integrity of their inquiry. Also, *Researcher Coach* provides researchers with an ample number of samples from actual published research (e.g., technical reports, doctoral dissertations, peer-reviewed professional articles) that will cement their understanding.

Chapter 1, Introduction to Research, set the foundational understanding of what is *research* as a construct and what it entails. Fundamentally, this chapter focused on the core notions of paradigm, ontology, epistemology, axiology, methodology, methods, and research questions—each one of which can be further disaggregated into components creating quite a complex system of knowledge that this chapter presents in clear and sequential manner.

Chapter 2, Writing the Introduction, guided the researcher through the writing of the components that set up the study. This chapter focuses on the formulation of the context for the research along the crucial elements that clearly communicate the phenomenon the study will address, what is known about it, and why it matters to further study it today. This chapter gave an understanding of how critical the context for research is and how much information needs to be known (hence, you demonstrate your level of expertise) in order to formulate a valid and sound inquiry.

Chapter 3, The Literature Review, showed researchers the process of writing and synthesizing relevant studies conducted by numerous researchers on the phenomenon of their scholarly interest. This is a very critical contextual piece for the research, and it follows a specific progressive sequence (e.g., writing an annotated bibliography). While anybody can summarize an article or more, the literature review is a far cry from such an approach. This component demands an exhaustive review of the current literature and the creation of a new system of knowledge about the phenomenon of the researcher's interest in which to situate the research as a logical next step. The researcher also must clearly determine what new understandings about the phenomenon the research will aim to provide.

Chapter 4, Methodology, presented the orchestration of all the tools necessary to successfully carry on the inquiry. This tool selection responds to many variables (e.g., paradigm, setting, participants), all of which must function as a robust articulated system. This system provides the technical quality assurance needed to demonstrate that the study is sound, will validly study the phenomenon of interest, and draw valid conclusions and recommendations for practice.

Chapter 5, Writing the Results, walked the researcher through the systematization of data analysis, visual presentation (i.e., tables, figures), and reporting of findings. All of these steps are devoid of personal or professional opinions; the writing needs to be objective and reflect what was actually obtained. Any changes to the original plan (e.g., addition of a data analysis technique) should be reported when writing the results. Quantitative and Qualitative data are analyzed, presented, and reported in significantly different manners and through quite different techniques. This chapter provided the researcher with an introduction to such processes.

Chapter 6, Writing the Discussion, detailed the writing of the components that wrap up the study. Fundamentally, this chapter helps the researcher understand how to provide an interpretation of the study's findings. This process requires that researchers' professional and research expertise, along with their knowledge of the subject matter, come into play jointly to give meaning to their discovery. Additionally, researchers need to clearly articulate directions for actionable recommendations to practitioners as well as researchers in this field of study.

Chapter 7, Qualitative Research Designs, described each one of the methodologies available to researchers when studying a phenomenon through a qualitative lens. It also guided researchers through the process of data analysis and narrative or visual data reporting in much more depth than the information provided in Chapter 5.

Chapter 8, Quantitative Research Designs, described each one of the methodologies available to researchers when studying a phenomenon through a quantitative lens. It also guided them through the process of data analysis and narrative or visual data reporting in much more depth than the information provided in Chapter 5.

Chapter 9, General Research Items, brought awareness of the inclusion and formatting of some additional components (e.g., appendix, dedication, acknowledgments, list of references, copyright page) that will be required depending how researchers are planning to make their research public (e.g., peer-reviewed manuscript, conference presentation, doctoral dissertation, thesis). This chapter also included a few tips that the authors have found quite important when engaging in scholarly writing.

Researcher Coach is a reflection of the authors' combined research experiences, which encompass a broad array of research endeavors (e.g., large-scale samples, quantitative research, qualitative research, mixed methods research, local studies, international studies, college students, graduate students, educational leaders, P–12 leaders, P–12 students, mainstream and minority populations). From these projects, the authors gained, and continue gaining, a large amount of knowledge and skills as well as dispositions to do research that is technically sound and significantly impacts the communities where these were conducted. It is the authors' goal that *Researcher Coach* will walk next to you as you embark on your next research endeavor!

REFERENCES

Abramson, G. (2015). Writing a dissertation proposal. *Journal of Applied Learning Technology, 5*(1), 6–13.

Ades, R. M. (2020). *A history and contemporary analysis of the standard adult high school program in Minnesota*. [Doctoral dissertation, Minnesota State University Moorhead]. RED. Dissertations, Theses, and Projects. https://red.mnstate.edu/cgi/viewcontent.cgi?article=1342&context=thesis

Adham, K. A., Ha, H., Mohd, S., & Yazid, Z. (2018). Learning to complete the PhD thesis. *Issues in Educational Research, 28*(4), 811–829.

Adom, D., Hussein, E. K., & Agyem, J. A. (2018). Theoretical and conceptual framework: Mandatory ingredients of a quality research. *International Journal of Scientific Research, 7*(1), 438–441.

Altman, D. G., & Bland, M. J. (2005). Standard deviations and standard errors. *BMJ, 331*, 903.

American Psychological Association. (2020). *Publication manual of the American Psychological Association: The official guide to APA style* (7th ed.). American Psychological Association.

Anderson, L. W., Krathwohl, D. R., & Bloom, B. S. (2001). A taxonomy for learning, teaching, and assessing: A revision of Bloom's taxonomy of educational objectives. Longman.

Antell, J., Blevins, A., Jensen, K., & Massey, G. (2002). *Residential and household poverty of American Indians on the Wind River Indian Reservation*. Laramie: University of Wyoming.

Antman E., Lau J., Kupelnick B., Mosteller F., & Chalmers T. (1992). A comparison of results of meta-analyses of randomized control trials and recommendations of clinical experts: Treatment for myocardial infarction. *JAMA 268*, 240–248.

Armstrong, P. (n.d.). Bloom's Taxonomy. *Vanderbilt University Center for Teaching*. https://cft.vanderbilt.edu/guides-sub-pages/blooms-taxonomy/

Arriola, L. E. (2012, 9 de diciembre). *Fórmulas de tamaño muestral* [video]. Youtube. https://www.youtube.com/watch?v=mraM5jEDO5s

Atkinson, L. Z., & Cipriani, A. (2018). How to carry out a literature search for a systematic review: A practical guide. *BJPsych Advances, 24,* 74–82. doi: 10.1192/bja.2017.3

Babchuck, W. A. (1996, October*). Glaser or Strauss?: Grounded theory and adult education.* In J. Dirkx (Ed.), Proceedings of the Fifteenth Annual Midwest Research-to Practice Conference in Adult, Continuing, and Community Education, Lincoln, Nebraska (ED477391). ERIC. https://files.eric .ed.gov/fulltext/ED477391.pdf

Bednall, J. (2006). Epoche and bracketing within the phenomenological paradigm. *Issues in Educational Research, 16,* 123–138. http://www.iier.org.au /iier16/bednall.html

Berman, J. (2013). Utility of a conceptual framework within doctoral study: A researcher's reflections. *Issues in Educational Research, 23*(1), 1–18.

Berthon, P., Nairn, A., & Money, A. (2003). Through the paradigm funnel: A conceptual tool for literature analysis. *Marketing Education Review, 13*(2), 55–66.

Bloland, H. G. (1995). Postmodernism and higher education. *Journal of Higher Education, 66,* 521–559.

Bockelmann, T. (2021). *The effects of a shared vision of teacher leadership on classroom teachers' instruction* [Doctoral dissertation, Minnesota State University Moorhead]. RED. Dissertations, Theses, and Projects. https://red .mnstate.edu/cgi/viewcontent.cgi?article=1495&context=thesis

Bradbury, B. L. (2005). *A qualitative study of the factors related to the academic success of American Indian students* [Doctoral dissertation, Capella University]. https://www.researchgate.net/profile/Boyd_Bradbury/pub lication/311453530_A_Qualitative_Study_of_the_Factors_Related_to_the _Academic_Success_of_American_Indian_Students/links/5847333508 ae8e63e6308c14/A-Qualitative-Study-of-the-Factors-Related-to-the -Academic-Success-of-American-Indian-Students.pdf

Bradbury, B. L. (2011a). The emergence of the customized on-site master's degree cohort model. Teacher action research in rural schools. *Thresholds in Education, XXXVII* (1–2). https://academyedstudies.files.wordpress.com /2015/09/2011completethrvol37no122.pdf

Bradbury, B. L. (2011b, February 10). *An autoethnographical account of a Midwesterner's travels in post-apartheid South Africa*. Ethnographic and Qualitative Research Conference, Las Vegas. https://www.eqrc.net/

Bradbury, B. L., Bergland, J., Bergman, J., Brown, D., Clark, T., Cole, L., Darmofal, L., Dobmeier, T., Howell, C., Lajimodiere, D., Moshier, T., Peterson, S., Phillips, A., Williams, B., & Wright, T. (2010*). Preliminary report: Comprehensive study of education on the* Patiño *Indian Reservation* [Research Report]. https://www.researchgate.net/publication/337441040_WE_Preliminary_Report_Phase_I

Bradbury, B. L., Suárez Sousa, X. P., Coquyt, M., Bockelmann, T. L., & Pahl, A. L. (2020). Teaching under crisis: Impact and implications of the COVID-19 pandemic on education in Minnesota. *The Interactive Journal of Global Leadership and Learning, 1*(2), 1–78.

Bradbury, B. L., Suárez Sousa, X., Tack, D., Cole, C., Phillips, A., Peterson, S., Wright, T., & Darmofal, L. M. (2012). *Comprehensive study of education and related services on the White Earth Indian Reservation: Phase II final report* [Research Report]. https://www.researchgate.net/publication/269333521_Comprehensive_Study_of_Education_and_Related_Services_on_the_White_Earth_Indian_Reservation_Phase_II_Copyright_2012

Brekken, A. K. (2021). *Preceptorship within accredited nutrition and dietetics programs: A pragmatic mixed methods study* [Doctoral dissertation, Minnesota State University Moorhead]. RED. Dissertations, Theses, and Projects. https://red.mnstate.edu/cgi/viewcontent.cgi?article=1510&context=thesis

Bremer, A. (2020). *How teachers of different content areas use and define rubrics* [Doctoral dissertation, Minnesota State University Moorhead]. RED. Dissertations, Theses, and Projects. https://red.mnstate.edu/cgi/viewcontent.cgi?article=1324&context=thesis

Brescia, W., & Fortune, J. C. (1988, March). *Standardized testing of American Indian students* (ED296813). ERIC. https://files.eric.ed.gov/fulltext/ED296813.pdf

Briggs, A. R. J., Coleman, M., & Morrison, M. (Eds.). (2012). *Research methods in educational leadership and management* (3rd ed.). SAGE Publications.

Brown, M. E. L., & Dueñas, A. N. (2020). A medical science educator's guide to selecting a research paradigm: Building a basis for better research. *Medical Science Educator, 30,* 545–553. https://link.springer.com/article/10.1007/s40670-019-00898-9

Burklund, A. (2020). *Syncing up on satisfaction: A mixed methods study exploring synchronous online classroom learning satisfaction in the corporate training environment* [Doctoral dissertation, Minnesota State University

Moorhead]. RED. Dissertations, Theses, and Projects. https://red.mnstate
.edu/thesis/314

Butler, R. G. (2014, April). *Exploratory versus confirmatory research*. ResearchGate. https://www.researchgate.net/publication/267058525_Explor
atory_vs_Confirmatory_Research

Caissie, L. T., Goggin, C., & Best, L. A. (2017). Graphs, tables, and scientific
illustrations: Visualisation as the science of seeing gerontology. *Canadian
Journal on Aging, 36*(4), 536–548.

Carlson, K. M. (2020). *Predicting and perceiving teacher effectiveness of novice teachers* [Doctoral dissertation, Minnesota State University Moorhead].
RED. Dissertations, Theses, and Projects. https://red.mnstate.edu/thesis/396/

Carr, J. E., & Burkholder, E. O. (1998, June). *Creating single-subject design
graphs with Microsoft Excel*. ResearchGate. https://www.researchgate.net
/publication/25099210_Creating_Single-Subject_Design_Graphs_With_Mi
crosoft_Excel

Carter, D. J. (2004, Winter). Editor's review of John U. Ogbu's Black American
students in an affluent suburb: A study of academic disengagement. *Harvard
Educational Review*. https://www.hepg.org/her-home/issues/harvard-educa
tional-review-volume-74-issue-4/herarticle/_38

Chandler J., Cumpston, M., Thomas, J., Higgins, J. P. T, Deeks, J. J., & Clarke,
M. J. (2019, August). Introduction. In: J. PT Higgins, J. Thomas, J. Chandler,
M. Cumpston, T. Li, M. J. Page, & V. A. Welch (Eds.), *Cochrane Handbook
for Systematic Reviews of Interventions* version 6.0. Cochrane. https://train
ing.cochrane.org/handbook/current/chapter-i

Cirks, K. (2021). *The road less traveled: An insight to the educational journeys of
American Indian students in higher education*. [Doctoral dissertation, Minnesota State University Moorhead]. RED. Dissertations, Theses, and Projects.
https://red.mnstate.edu/cgi/viewcontent.cgi?article=1520&context=thesis

Constable, R., Cowell, M., Zornek Crawford, S., Golden, D., Hartvigsen, J.,
Morgan, K., Mudgett, A., Parrish, K., Thomas, L., Yolanda Thompson, E.,
Turner, R., & Palmquist, M. (n.d.) *Ethnography, observational research, and
narrative inquiry*. Writing@CSU. Colorado State University. https://writing
.colostate.edu/guides/guide.cfm?guideid=63

Coquyt, M. (2019). The effects of service-learning on the moral development
of college students. *The Interactive Journal of Global Leadership and Learning, 1*(2), 1–37.

Creswell, J. W. (1998). *Qualitative inquiry and research design: Choosing
among five traditions*. SAGE Publications.

Creswell, J. W. (2003). *Research design: Qualitative, quantitative, and mixed
methods approaches* (2nd ed.). SAGE Publications.

Creswell, J. W. (2014). *Research design: Qualitative, quantitative and mixed methods* (4th ed.). SAGE Publications.

Creswell, J. W., & Clark, P. V. L. (2011). *Designing and conducting mixed methods research* (2nd ed.). SAGE Publications.

Creswell, J. W., & Plano Clark, V. L. (2007). *Designing and conducting mixed methods research*. SAGE Publications.

Creswell, J. W., & Poth, C. N. (2018). *Qualitative inquiry & research design: Choosing among five approaches* (4th ed.). SAGE Publications.

Cummings, P. (2020). *Surviving in school: A correlational study on teachers' social emotional learning, self-efficacy, and response to students' challenging behaviors* [Doctoral dissertation, Minnesota State University Moorhead]. RED. Dissertations, Theses, and Projects. https://red.mnstate.edu/cgi/view content.cgi?article=1409&context=thesis

Dass, M. (2020). *Diagramming academic equity: Exploring educator percep- tions of using student data to institute equitable academic programming in public secondary schools.* [Doctoral dissertation, Minnesota State University Moorhead]. RED. Dissertations, Theses, and Projects. https://red.mnstate .edu/thesis/380/

DeCoker, G. (2009). How to get a teaching job at a liberal-arts college. *Chron- icle of Higher Education, 56*(17). https://www.chronicle.com/article/how-to -get-a-teaching-job-at-a-liberal-arts-college/

Denzin, N. K., & Lincoln, Y. S. (2000). Reconstructing the relationships be- tween universities and society through action research. In N. K. Denzin & Y. S. Lincoln (Eds.), *Handbook of qualitative research* (2nd ed., pp. 367– 378). SAGE Publications.

Denzin, N. K., & Lincoln, Y. S. (2003). *The landscape of qualitative research: Theories and issues* (2nd ed.). SAGE Publications.

Dimitrov, D., Rumrill, P., Fitzgerald, & Hennessey, M. (2001, February). Reli- ability in rehabilitation measurement. ResearchGate. https://www.research gate.net/publication/11027779_Reliability_in_rehabilitation_measurement

Faryadi, Q. (2019). PhD thesis writing process: A systematic approach—how to write your methodology, results and conclusion. *Creative Education, 10,* 766–783.

Fay, B. (1987). *Critical social science.* Cornell University Press.

Field, A. (2009). *Discovering Statistics Using SPSS* (3rd ed.). SAGE Publications.

Fielding, N. (2002). Automating the ineffable: qualitative software and the meaning of qualitative research, in May, T. (Ed.). *Qualitative Research in Action.* SAGE Publications.

Florey, J., & Tafoya, N. (1988). *Identifying gifted and talented American Indian students: An overview* (ED296810). ERIC. https://eric.ed.gov/?id=ED296810

Foucault, M. (1977). *Discipline and punish: The birth of the prison*. Penguin.

Fraenkel, J. R., Wallen, N.E., & Hyun, H. H. (2019). *How to design and evaluate research in education* (10th ed.). McGraw Hill Education.

Frels, R. K., Onwuegbuzie, A. J., & Slate, J. R. (2010). Editorial: A step-by-step guide for creating tables. *Research in the Schools*, *17*(2), xxxviii–lix.

Galdone, P. (1970). *The three little pigs*. Houghton Mifflin/Clarion Books.

Gamson, J. (2000). Sexualities, queer theory, and qualitative research. In N. K. Denzin & U. S. Lincoln (Eds.), *Handbook of qualitative research* (2nd ed., pp. 347–365). SAGE Publications.

Gillette, J. M. (1927). Nature and limits of social phenomena. *Social Forces*, *5*(4), 561–571.

Glaser, B. G., & Strauss, A. L. (1967). *The discovery of grounded theory: Strategies for qualitative research*. Aldine Transaction.

Glaser, B. G., & Strauss, A. L. (1999). *The discovery of grounded theory: Strategies for qualitative research*. Aldine De Gruyter.

Grant, C., & Osanloo, A. (2014). Understanding, selecting, and integrating a theoretical framework in dissertation research: Creating the blueprint for your "house." *Administrative Issues Journal*, *4*(2), 12–26.

Gray, D. E. (2018). *Doing research in the real world* (4th ed.). SAGE Publications.

Greenwood, D. J., & Levin, M. (2000). Reconstructing the relationships between universities and society through action research. In N. K. Denzin & U. S. Lincoln (Eds.), *Handbook of qualitative research* (2nd ed., pp. 85–106). SAGE Publications.

Grogan, M., & Cleaver Simmons, J. M. (2012). Taking a critical stance in research. In A. R. Briggs, M. Coleman, & M. Morrison (Eds.), *Research methods in educational leadership & management* (pp. 122–139). SAGE Publications.

Gubrium, J. F., & Holstein, J. A. (2000). Analyzing interpretive practice. In N. K. Denzin & U. S. Lincoln (Eds.), *Handbook of qualitative research* (2nd ed.) (pp. 85–106). SAGE Publications.

Hassani, H., Ghodsi, M., & Howell, G. (2010). A note on standard deviation and standard error. *Teaching Mathematics and Its Applications*, *29*, 108–112.

Heydebrand, W. V. (2001). Structuralism, theories of. *International Encyclopedia of the Social and Behavioral Sciences*, 15230–15233. https://doi.org/10.1016/B0-08-043076-7/01976-8

Hibberts, M. F., & Burke Johnson, R. (2012). Mixed methods research. In A. R. Briggs, M. Coleman, & M. Morrison (Eds.), *Research methods in educational leadership & management* (pp. 122–139). SAGE Publications.

Higgins, J. P. T., & Thomas, J. (2019). *Cochrane handbook for systematic reviews of interventions* (2nd ed.). Cochrane.

Hinchey, P. H. (2008). *Action research*. Peter Lang.

Honetschlager, V. (2020a). *The impact of a freshman academy on academic achievement and engagement* [Doctoral dissertation, Minnesota State University Moorhead]. RED. Dissertations, Theses, and Projects. Minnesota State University Moorhead. https://red.mnstate.edu/cgi/viewcontent .cgi?article=1434&context=thesis

Honetschlager, V. (2020b). Bridging the high school transition: Assessing the impact of a freshman academy on student success. *The Interactive Journal of Global Leadership and Learning, 1*(2).

Hostetler, A. J., & Herdt, G. H. (1998). Culture, sexual lifeways, and development subjectivities; Rethinking sexual taxonomies. *Social Research, 65*(2), 249–290.

Howell, D. C. (2004). *Fundamental statistics for the behavioral sciences* (5th ed.). Thompson.

Hsieh, H., & Shannon, S. E. (2005). Three approaches to qualitative content analysis. *Qualitative Health Research, 15*(9), 1277–1288.

Huck, S. W. (2000). *Reading statistics and research* (3rd ed.). Addison Wesley Longman.

Instituto de Estudios Peruanos (2021). *Reporte Técnico: Encuesta de Intención de Voto—Elecciones Generales 2021, Segunda Vuelta* (Abril II 2021). Instituto de Estudios Peruanos. https://iep.org.pe/wp-content/uploads/2021/04 /Informe-Tecnico-IEP-OP-Abril-II-2021.pdf

Jager, J., Putnick, D. L., & Bornstein, M. H. (2017). More than just convenient: The scientific merits of homogeneous convenience samples. *Monographs of the Society for Research in Child Development, 82*(2), 13–30.

Johnson, R. B., & Christensen, L. (2017). *Educational research: Quantitative, qualitative, and mixed approaches* (6th ed.). SAGE Publications.

Jones, A. (2015, January 7). *These are very similar terms and as such there is hardly any difference between them. Overall researchers tend to adopt research* [Comment on the online forum post: *What are the differences between conceptual framework and theoretical framework?*] ResearchGate. https:// www.researchgate.net/post/What-are-the-differences-between-conceptual -framework-and-theoretical-framework

Kallet, R. H. (2004). How to write the methods section of a research paper. *Respiratory Care, 49*, 10, 1229–1232.

Kivunja, C. (2018). Distinguishing between theory, theoretical framework, and conceptual framework: A systematic review of lessons from the field. *International Journal of Higher Education, 7*(6), 44–53.

Kivunja, C., & Kuyini, A. B. (2017). Understanding and applying paradigms in educational contexts. *International Journal of Higher Education, 6*(5), 26–41.

Knaflic, C. N. (2015). *Storytelling with data: A data visualization guide for business professionals*. Wiley.

Knaub, J. R. (2017, December 5). How can I calculate the proper sample size in convenient sampling? [Online forum post]. ResearchGate. https://www.researchgate.net/post/How_can_I_calculate_the_proper_sample_size_in_convenient_sampling

Kowalewski, H. (2017). Why neurolinguistics needs first-person methods. *Language Sciences, 64,* 167–179.

Kratochwill, T. R., Hitchcock, J., Horner, R. H., Levin, J. R., Odom, S. L., Rindskopf, D. M., & Shadish, W. R. (2010). Single-case designs technical documentation. What Works Clearinghouse. http://ies.ed.gov/ncee/wwc/pdf/wwc_scd.pdf

Kristjansson-Nelson, K. (2020a). *The theory of dispositions in filmmaking and leadership* [Doctoral dissertation, Minnesota State University Moorhead]. RED. Dissertations, Theses, and Projects. https://red.mnstate.edu/cgi/viewcontent.cgi?article=1323&context=thesis

Kristjansson-Nelson, K. (2020b). Methods in practice: Grounded theory in media arts education research. *The Interactive Journal of Global Leadership and Learning, 1*(1). https://red.mnstate.edu/cgi/viewcontent.cgi?article=1002&context=ijgll

Kuhn, G. S. (1962). *The structure of scientific revolutions*. The University of Chicago.

Ladson-Billings, G. (1997). Just what is critical race theory and what's it doing in a nice field like education? *Qualitative Studies in Education, 2*(1), 7–24. https://www.researchgate.net/publication/233153707_Just_What_is_Critical_Race_Theory_and_What%27s_It_Doing_in_a_Nice_Field_Like_Education

Larson, L. K. (2020). *Uncertainty in Academia: A mixed methods study identifying how value statements on plagiarism correlate with plagiarism reporting behaviors of undergraduate faculty in a distance education program* [Doctoral dissertation, Minnesota State University Moorhead]. RED. Dissertations, Theses, and Projects. https://red.mnstate.edu/cgi/viewcontent.cgi?article=1320&context=thesis

Lawshe, C. H. (1975, July 18). *A quantitative approach to content validity* [Paper presentation]. Content Validity II, Bowling Green State University. https://doi.org/10.1111/j.1744-6570.1975.tb01393.x

Leland, A. (2020). *Full service community school intervention: Case study of Somali parent–school engagement within a rural mid-western school district* [Doctoral dissertation, Minnesota State University Moorhead]. RED. Dissertations, Theses, and Projects. https://red.mnstate.edu/cgi/viewcontent.cgi?article=1344&context=thesis

Lundberg, I. (2020). *Exclusionary discipline disparities: A case study* [Doctoral dissertation, Minnesota State University Moorhead]. RED. Dissertations, Theses, and Projects. https://red.mnstate.edu/cgi/viewcontent.cgi?article=1366&context=thesis

Manikandan, S. (2011). Measures of dispersion. *Journal of Pharmacology & Pharmacotherapeutics, 2*(4), 315–316.

Mason, J. (2018). *Qualitative researching* (3rd ed.). SAGE Publications.

Matthiessen, C., & Kashyap, A. K. (2014). The construal of space in different registers: An exploratory study. *Language Sciences, 45*, 1–27.

Maxwell, J. A. (2013). *Qualitative research design: An interactive approach.* SAGE Publications.

McMahon, E. (2021). *Designing effective online courses: Exploring the relationships among teaching self-efficacy, professional development, faculty experience, and implementation of effective online course design practices* [Unpublished doctoral dissertation]. Minnesota State University Moorhead.

Merriam-Webster. (n.d.) Full definition of appendix. https://www.merriam-webster.com/dictionary/appendix

Mertler, C. A. (2020). *Action research: Improving schools and empowering educators* (6th ed.). SAGE Publications.

Miles, D. A. (2019, June). *Research methods and strategies: Let's stop the madness Part 2: Understanding the difference between limitations vs delimitations.* ResearchGate. https://www.researchgate.net/publication/334279571_ARTICLE_Research_Methods_and_Strategies_Let%27s_Stop_the_Madness_Part_2_Understanding_the_Difference_Between_Limitations_vs_Delimitations

Moaddab, P. (2014). Why and when passive voice. *Journal of Novel Applied Sciences, 3*(12), 1423–1418.

Morales-Bermudez, F. (2011). *The scientific problem: Logic, philosophy, planning, and development.* Fondo Editorial Universidad de Lima.

Morrison, M. (2012). Understanding methodology. In A. R. Briggs, M. Coleman, & M. Morrison (Eds.), *Research methods in educational leadership & management* (pp. 14–27). SAGE Publications.

Morrow, R. A., & Brown, D. D. (1994). *Critical theory and methodology.* SAGE Publications.

Mujis, D. (2012). Surveys and sampling. In A. R. Briggs, M. Coleman, & M. Morrison (Eds.), *Research methods in educational leadership & management* (pp. 140–154). SAGE Publications.

Nagy, Hesse-Biber, S., & Leavy, P. (2011). *The practice of qualitative research* (2nd ed.). SAGE Publications.

National Institutes of Health. (2021). Protecting Human Research Participants: NIH Office of Extramural Research. https://grants.nih.gov/sites/default/files/PHRP_Archived_Course_Materials_English.pdf

Navarro, I. (2020, September 15). [Lecture notes on resource allocation]. Cursos de Capacitación, Pontificia Universidad Católica del Perú. https://paideia.pucp.edu.pe

Nel, J. P. (2016, October 16). Research paradigms: Structuralism. ¡Ntgrty. https://www.intgrty.co.za/2016/10/10/research-paradigms-structuralism/

Newman, I., & Covrig, D. M. (2013). Writer's Forum: Building consistency between title, problem statement, purpose, & research questions to improve the quality of research plans and reports. *New Horizons in Adult Education & Human Resource Development*, 25(1), 70–79.

Nikitina, L. (2015, January 19). *I also have to have both theoretical and conceptual frameworks in my study. From my reading of literature on research* [Comment on the online forum post *What are the differences between conceptual framework and theoretical framework?*] ResearchGate. https://www.researchgate.net/post/What-are-the-differences-between-conceptual-framework-and-theoretical-framework

Norman, G. R., & Streiner, D. L. (2008). *Biostatistics: The bare essentials* (3rd ed.). BC Decker Inc.

Northcentral University Library. (2020, September 9). Finding seminal works. https://ncu.libguides.com/researchprocess/seminalworks

Northern Arizona University. (2020). Biography. https://jan.ucc.nau.edu/~jar/Bio.html

O'Connell, K. (2020). *Summer literacy academy: Evaluating the impact of supports, book choice, incentives, and a focused, literacy-based summer learning program on reading outcomes for rural, middle school students* [Doctoral dissertation, Minnesota State University Moorhead]. RED. Dissertations, Theses, and Projects. https://red.mnstate.edu/cgi/viewcontent.cgi?article=1397&context=thesis

Ogbu, J. (1990, Winter). Minority education in comparative perspective. *The Journal of Negro Education*, 59(1), 45–57.

Oleson, V. (1994). Feminisms and models of qualitative research. In N. K. Denzin & U. S. Lincoln (Eds.), *Handbook of qualitative research* (pp. 158–174). SAGE Publications.

Olssen, M. (2003). Structuralism, post-structuralism, neo-liberalism: Assessing Foucault's legacy. *Journal of Education Policy*, 18(2), 189–202.

Otto, M. (2019, October 4). How to build a conceptual framework in qualitative research? [Online forum post]. https://www.researchgate.net/post

/How_to_build_a_conceptual_framework_in_qualitative_research#view=5d ff0c5ab93ecd2c6210d53c

Oxman, A., & Guyatt, G. (1993). The science of reviewing research. *Annals of the New York Academy of Sciences, 703*, 125–133.

Patel, S. (2015, July 15). The research paradigm—methodology, epistemology, and ontology—explained in simple language [Web log post]. http:salmapatel .co.uk/academia/the-research-paradigm-methodology-epistemology-and-on tology-explained-in-simple-language

Patiño, C. M., & Ferreira, J. C. (2018). Inclusion and exclusion criteria in research studies: Definitions and why they matter. *Brazilian Journal of Pulmonology, 44*(2), 84.

Pedersen, M. J., & Stritch, J. M. (2018). RNICE Model: Evaluating the contribution of replication studies in public administration and management research. *Public Administration Review, 78*(4), 606–612.

Pemberton, C. L. A. (2012). A "how-to" guide for the education thesis/dissertation process. *Kappa Delta Pi Record, 48*, 82–86.

Perryman, J. (2012). Discourse analysis. In A. R. Briggs, M. Coleman, & M. Morrison (Eds.), *Research methods in educational leadership & management* (pp. 309–322). SAGE Publications.

Pilishvili, T., Fleming-Dutra, K. E., Farrar, J. L., Gierke, R., Mohr, N. M., Talan, D. A., Krishnadasan, A., Harland, K. K., Smithline, H. A., Hou, H. A., Lee, L. C., Lim, S. C., Moran, G. J., Krebs, E., Steele, M., Beiser, D. G., Faine, B., Haran, J. P., Nandi, U., . . . Vaccine Effectiveness Among Healthcare Personnel Study Team. (2021, May 14). Interim estimates of vaccine effectiveness of Pfizer-BioNTech and Moderna COVID-19 vaccines among health care personnel—33 US sites. *Centers for Disease Control and Prevention–Morbidity and Mortality Weekly Report (MMWR), 70*, 1–6. https://www.cdc.gov/mmwr/volumes/70/wr/pdfs/mm7020e2-H.pdf

Pink, S., Horst, H., Postill, J., Lewis, T., & Tacchi, J. (2016). *Digital ethnographies: Principles and practice.* SAGE Publications.

Punch, K. F. (2011). *Introduction to research methods in education.* SAGE Publications.

Purdue Online Writing Lab. (n.d.). Annotated bibliography samples. https:// owl.english.purdue.edu/owl/resource/614/03/

Reyhner, J. (1992). *Plans for dropout prevention and special school support services for American Indian and Alaska Native students* (ED343762). ERIC. https://files.eric.ed.gov/fulltext/ED343762.pdf

Reyhner, J. (1993). American Indian language policy and school success. *The Journal of Educational Issues of Language Minority Students, 12*(*III*), 35–39. http://jan.ucc.nau.edu/~jar/BOISE.html

Roberts, C., and Hyatt, L. (2019). *The dissertation journey* (3rd ed.). Corwin.

Rudestam, K. E., & Newton, R. R. (2014). *Surviving your dissertation*. SAGE Publications.

Sampson, J. P. (2017). *A guide to quantitative and qualitative dissertation research* (2nd ed.). Florida State University College of Education. https://diginole.lib.fsu.edu/islandora/object/fsu:207241/datastream/PDF/view

Save the Children. (2002). *America's forgotten children: Child poverty in rural America* (ED 567475). ERIC. https://files.eric.ed.gov/fulltext/ED467475.pdf

Scotland, J. (2012). Exploring the philosophical underpinnings of research: Relating ontology and epistemology to the methodology and methods of the scientific, interpretive, and critical research. *Canadian Center of Science and Education*, 5(9), 9–16.

Scott, D. (2012). Research design: Frameworks, strategies, methods and technologies. In A. R. Briggs, M. Coleman, & M. Morrison (Eds.), *Research methods in educational leadership & management* (pp. 122–139). SAGE Publications.

Scott, D., & Morrison, M. (2006). *Key ideas in educational research*. Continuum.

Shannon, R. A., Bergren, M. D., & Matthews, A. (2010). Frequent visitors: Somatization in school-age children and implications for nurses. *The Journal of School Nursing, 26*(3), 169–182.

Sheskin, D. J. (2000). *Handbook of parametric and nonparametric statistical procedures* (2nd ed.). Chapman & Hall/CRC. https://fmipa.umri.ac.id/wp-content/uploads/2016/03/David_J._Sheskin_David_Sheskin_Handbook_of_ParaBookFi.org_.pdf

Silliman, E. R., Bahr, R. H., & Wilkinson, L. C. (2019). Writing across the academic languages: Introduction. *Reading and Writing, 33*, 1–11.

Simon, M. K. (2011). *Dissertation and scholarly research: Recipes for success*. Dissertation Success, LLC.

Simons, H. (2009). *Case study research in practice*. SAGE Publications.

Šimundić, A. (2013). Bias in research. *Biochemia Medica, 23*(1), 12–15.

Slife, B. D., & Williams, R. N. (1995). *What's behind the research? Discovering hidden assumptions in the behavioral sciences*. SAGE Publications.

Streiner, D. L. (2007). A shortcut to rejection: How not to write the results section of a paper. *The Canadian Journal of Psychiatry, 52*(6), 385–389. https://journals.sagepub.com/doi/pdf/10.1177/070674370705200608

Stringer, E. T. (2007). *Action research* (3rd ed.). SAGE Publications.

Suárez Sousa, X. (2021). Scales of measurement [PowerPoint Slides]. Brightspace. https://mnstate.learn.minnstate.edu

Swisher, K. (1991). *American Indian/Alaskan Native learning styles: Research and practice* (ED 335175). ERIC. https://files.eric.ed.gov/fulltext/ED335175.pdf

Tedlock, B. (2000). Ethnography and ethnographic representation. In N. K. Denzin & Y. S. Lincoln (Eds.), *Handbook of qualitative research* (2nd ed., pp. 455–486). SAGE Publications.

Tenforde, M. W., Olson, S. M., Self, W. H., Talbot, H. K., Lindsell, C. J., Steingrub, J. S., Shapiro, N. I., Ginde, A. A., Douin, D. J., Prekker, M. E., Brown, S. M., Peltan, I. D., Gong, M. N., Mohamed, A., Khan, A., Exline, M. C., Files, D. C., Gibbs, K. W., Stubblefield, W. B., . . . HAIVEN Investigators. (2021, May 7). Effectiveness of Pfizer-BioNTech and Moderna vaccines against COVID-19 among hospitalized adults aged ≥ 65 years—United States. *Centers for Disease Control and Prevention–Morbidity and Mortality Weekly Report (MMWR)*, *70*(18), 674–679. https://www.cdc.gov/mmwr/volumes/70/wr/mm7018e1.htm?s_cid=mm7018e1_w

Thomas, J. (1993). *Doing critical ethnography*. SAGE Publications.

Tomar, B. (2014, March–April). Axiology in teacher education: Implementation and challenges. *IOSR Journal of Research & Method in Education*, *4*(2, Ver. III), 51–54. https://www.iosrjournals.org/iosr-jrme/papers/Vol-4%20Issue-2/Version-3/H04235154.pdf

Tuñón, J., & Brydges, B. (2006). A study of using rubrics and citation analysis to measure the quality of doctoral dissertation reference lists from traditional and nontraditional institution. *Journal of Library Administration*, *45*(3–4), 459–481.

USC Libraries. (2021). *The abstract.* https://libguides.usc.edu/writingguide/abstract

van Manen, M. (1990). *Researching lived experience: Human science for an action sensitive pedagogy.* The University of Western Ontario.

Walker, L. S., Beck, J. E., Garber, J., & Lambert, W. (2009). Children's somatization inventory: Psychometric properties of the Revised Form (CSI-24). *Journal of Pediatric Psychology*, *34*(4), 430–440.

Wiersma, W. (1995). *Research methods in education: An introduction.* Allyn and Bacon.

Zettle, R. D. (2020). Treatment manuals, single-subject designs, and evidence-based practice: A clinical behavioral analytic perspective. *The Psychological Record*, *70*, 649–658.

INDEX

Page references for figures are italicized.

abstract, 182–83
academic writing, 21, 27, 66, 186
acknowledgements, 182
action research, 16–17
alternative hypothesis, 35, 124, 128, 139, 178
annotated bibliography, 54–55, 64, 66
appendix, 184–85
axiology, 3, 5–8

bar graph, 157, *158*
bias, *4*, 7, 46, 93, 104, 131. *See also* epoché
Bloom's taxonomy, 8, 62
boxplot, 156–57, 162, 165

case study, 141–42
census, 81
coding, 103, 139, 144–51. *See also* data analysis

conceptual framework, 28, 30–32, 37, 57, 66, 101
confidence interval, 105, 177
confirmatory study, 154, 175, 177
constitutive definition of variables, 94
construct, 37
constructivism. *See* interpretivism
copyright page, 181
correlation coefficient, 160
critical theory, 3, *4–6*, 10, 13, 16, 73
curriculum vitae, 185

data: preparation of, 104; qualitative representation, 102, 109–12; quantitative representation, 104, 113–17
data analysis, 67, 70, 92; axial, 124, 145–46, 149–50; content analysis, 93; data analysis spiral, 145–47; deductive, 144, 147–48; inductive,

144, 147–48; open, 145–47, 149–50. *See also* coding
dedication, 182
deductive approach, 139
degrees of freedom, 105
delimitations, 40–41, 125–27; definition of, 125
demographic information, 100, 110
descriptive statistics, 82, 93, 105, 114, 172–74, 178
descriptive test, 114
discourse analysis, 18–19
discussion, 119; implications for change, 127; interpretation of findings, 120, 123–24; overview of the study, 120, 121–23; recommendations for action, 119, 128–30; recommendations for further study, 120, 130–31; researcher's reflection, 131

effect size, 176–77
emic perspective, 103
empiricism. *See* positivism
epistemology, 3, 5–8, 133–34; definition of 6, 72
epoché (bracketing), 138; definition of, 7
ethics, 39; confidentiality, 93; training, 80
ethnography, 15, 135–37
etic perspective, 103
exclusion criteria, 80–81, 85
exploratory study, 154
expository discourse, 21

feminism, 10, 13, 19
figures, 101, 106–18
Foucault, Michael, 11, 18
frequency polygon, 173

generalizability, 40, 85, 155, 169, 174; definition of, 67
Google Scholar, 56
grounded theory, 15, 110, 139–40, 149, 151

histogram, 157–158, 162, 165, 173
hypothesis, 3, 34, 67; alternative hypothesis, 35; construction of, 35; definition, 94; null hypothesis, 35, 93, 101, 105, 139, 142, 174, 178; testing, 177–179

inclusion criteria, 40, 80–81, 85
inductive approach, 139, 144
inferential statistics, 70, 93, 174–79
inferential test, 105, 114, 115
Institutional Review Board (IRB), 39
instrumentation, 86–92
interpretivism, 4–5, 8–9, 72–74, 82, 93, 136, 138, 142

keywords, 25
knowledge gap, 25

Laerd Statistics, 186
limitations, 40–41, 125–27; definition of, 125
line graph, 157, 158–59
literature review, 22, 24, 43–66, 68, 154; cognitive contemplation, 45; gap, 68; narrative review, 46; peer-reviewed, 43, 55, 65; primary sources, 25, 37, 65; purpose, 43–45; relevance, 53; saturation point, 65; search avenues, 55–59; secondary sources, 25, 37, 65; seminal works, 43, 51–52; synthesis of, 62–65, 66; systematic review, 46; tips, 65–66

measures of central tendency, 105
measures of variability, 105
methodology, 3, 5–8, 34, 66–72;
   alignment, 95–96; definition of,
   14; procedures, 67, 95. *See also*
   research question
member checks, 104
methods, 3, 5–8, 68, 71, 73;
   definition of, 14
mixed methods, 10, 15–18

narrative inquiry, 137
need for the study, 25
non-parametric, 105, 115, 174–76

objectivism, 72–74
ontology, 3, 5–8, 133–34, 136;
   definition of, 6, 71; operational
   definition, 37, 94; outliers, 157

paradigm: definition of, 2–6;
   paradigm funnel, 25
parameter, definition of, 169
parametric, 176
participants, 40, 78–81;
   demographics, 79, 82; target
   population, 85. *See also* sampling
phenomenology, 3, 16, 103, 138–39
phenomenon: definition of, 68; of
   interest, 22–23, 154, 164; results
   of, 99
pie chart, 157, 162–63, 165, 173
population, 81; target population, 85
positionality, 154. *See also* bias
positivism, 3–6, 8–9, 72–74, 83, 92,
   153
postmodernism, 3, 11, 12, 19, 26
post-positivism, 9
post-structuralism, 9, 11–13, 18. *See
   also* postmodernism

pragmatism, *4–5*, 8, 10–11, 73–74
primary sources, 25
procedures, 95
purpose of the study, 32–34, 68–69,
   143; descriptive, 143; explanatory,
   143; exploratory, 143; interpretive,
   143; road map, 33. *See also*
   statement of the problem

queer theory, 13
quotes, 103

realism, 72–74
reference list, 66, 183–84
register, 21
relevance of study, 23
relativism, 72–74
reliability, 89, 91–92, 97, 164
research: definition of, 1; paradigm, 29
research design, 71–76, 142, 134,
   153, 178; causal-comparative,
   162–63; correlational, 73–75,
   153–54, 160–61; cross-sectional
   research, 167; experimental,
   154–57; longitudinal, 167;
   quasi-experimental, 157–58;
   retrospective, 167; single-subject,
   158–60; survey, 14, 163–65
research paradigm, 71–73
research question, 2, 7, 67, 69, 70;
   alignment of, 96; construction of,
   34–37, 94–95
researcher bias, 93
ResearchGate, 56–58
results, 99–102
return rate, 165

sample, definition of, 81
sample size, 67, 82–83, 169–71;
   calculation of, 83

sampling, 67, 81–85, 168–74;
   convenience, 165, 168, 170;
   exclusion criteria, 80; inclusion
   criteria, 80; non-random (non-
   probabilistic), 84–85, 168;
   procedures, 81–82, 84; purposeful,
   165, 168; random, 84–85, 157,
   165, 166, 168, 170
scatterplot, 161, 165
secondary sources, 25
setting, 77
signature page, 181
significance level, 178–79
significance of the study, 24, 38,
   101
standard error, 168, 177
statement of the problem, 26–28, 32,
   67–68
statistic, definition of, 169
statistical assumptions, 175–76
Statistical Packet for the Social
   Sciences (SPSS), 93, 170
stem-and-leaf plot, 157, 162, 173
structuralism, 11–12, 18
Subject Matter Experts, 164
subjectivism, 4–5, 8, 72–74, 134

tables, 101, 106–18
theoretical framework, 28–32, 37, 66,
   101, 164

theoretical perspective, 3, 5–6;
   definition of, 9
theory, definition of, 28
thick description, 104; setting, 77,
   155, 159
topical outline, 60–61, 64, 66
transferability, 104
triangulation, 101
trustworthiness (credibility), 92, 104,
   136
Type I Error, 178
Type II Error, 178

validity, 67, 89–90, 92, 97, 164;
   definition of, 89; external, 85, 92,
   153, 155 165–66, 178; internal, 85,
   89, 153, 155, 165–66, 178
variability, measures of, 105
variables, 94; categorical, 87;
   constitutive, 94; continuous, 87,
   161; defining, 37; demographic,
   37, 163; dependent, 86, 158,
   160; independent, 86, 158,
   160; interval, 87; nominal, 87;
   operational, 37, 94; ordinal, 87;
   outcome, 160, 162; predictor
   (criterion), 160, 162; ratio, 87
very relevant literature, 24
voice: active, 186; participant, 103;
   passive, 168; researcher, 103

ABOUT THE AUTHORS

Ximena Suárez Sousa is professor of educational leadership at Minnesota State University Moorhead (MSUM). She is coordinator of the educational leadership doctoral degree program and managing editor of the *Interactive Journal of Global Leadership and Learning*. Dr. Suárez-Sousa holds a BS in psychology, an MEd in special education, and a PhD in curriculum and instruction from the University of Louisville. As an educational psychologist in her native Peru, Dr. Suárez-Sousa delivered applied behavioral analysis interventions to P–12 students with severe disabilities, provided counseling and training to families, and focused her research on parental stress and the validation of Spanish-translated psychoeducational assessment tools. Dr. Suárez-Sousa has worked in academia for about two decades; she was the coordinator of the MS degree in special education and teacher education assessment and the accreditation data manager at MSUM. She was also the site visitor and evaluator for the Council for the Accreditation of Educator Preparation (CAEP). Her research focuses on the development of local academic norms for psychoeducational assessment tools, validity and reliability determination, program impact evaluation, and issues related to online adult learning. Most of her research is conducted within the post-positivist paradigm, with survey research as her preferred methodology.

Boyd Bradbury is a professor of educational leadership and curriculum and instruction at Minnesota State University Moorhead (MSUM), where he is chair of leadership and learning, coordinator of the MS and EdS degrees in educational leadership, and editor-in-chief of the *Interactive Journal of Global Leadership and Learning*. He holds a BA and MAT in Spanish, an EdS in educational leadership, and a PhD in general education. Dr. Bradbury taught high school Spanish, was a secondary-school principal and superintendent, and held academic and graduate studies deanships at MSUM. Dr. Bradbury presents at regional, state, national, and international conferences and has twice been a visiting lecturer at Belarusian National Technical University. He has numerous publications to his credit, and his research focuses on educational leadership, pedagogy, academic achievement, teacher preparation and professional development, indigenous populations, demographics, diversity, distance education, and organizational structure and behavior. Dr. Bradbury has received various rewards, which include the 2002 Bemidji State University Outstanding Alumni Award; the 2017 Excellence in Service Award at MSUM (for his efforts to secure a $3 million appropriation from the Minnesota legislature to provide increased teacher credentialing to meet higher learning commission faculty requirements for high school teachers who teach concurrent enrollment courses); a 2019 induction into the Bemidji State University Professional Education Hall of Fame (which honors alumni who demonstrate excellence in teaching students or managing schools); and the 2019 Minnesota Rural Education Association Distinguished Service Award.